Penguin Critical Studies
Joint Advisory Editors:
Stephen Coote and Bryan Loughrey

William Shakespeare

As You Like It

A dramatic commentary

Peter Reynolds

Penguin Books

PENGUIN BOOKS

Published by the Penguin Group
27 Wrights Lane, London W8 5TZ, England
Viking Penguin Inc., 40 West 23rd Street, New York, New York 10010, USA
Penguin Books Australia Ltd, Ringwood, Victoria, Australia
Penguin Books Canada Ltd, 2801 John Street, Markham, Ontario, Canada L3R 1B4
Penguin Books (NZ) Ltd, 182–190 Wairau Road, Auckland 10, New Zealand

Penguin Books Ltd, Registered Offices: Harmondsworth, Middlesex, England

Published in Penguin Books 1988

Made and printed in Great Britain by
Richard Clay Ltd, Bungay, Suffolk
Filmset in 9 on 11pt Monophoto Times

For Polly

One of the reasons why Shakespeare continues to be performed is not that there *is* a central realizable intention in each play that we still continue to value, but because we are still looking for the possibility of unforeseen meanings.

Jonathan Miller, *Subsequent Performances*

Contents

Acknowledgements

Acknowledgements

I am grateful to the Shakespeare Centre Library, Royal Shakespeare Theatre Collections, for permission to reproduce an extract from the Royal Shakespeare Company's prompt-copy of Terry Hands's 1980 production of *As You Like It*. I should also like to thank the staff of that excellent and hospitable library located at the Shakespeare Birthplace Trust in Stratford-upon-Avon. I am in debt to my colleagues and friends at the Roehampton Institute and in particular to Susanne Greenhalgh and Neil Taylor. Dr Jim Davis, of the Department of Theatre Studies, University of New South Wales, Australia, kindly loaned me two unpublished articles on *As You Like It*, both of which I found absolutely invaluable. Dr Stephen Coote, co-editor of the Critical Studies series, read my manuscript, as did Sonia Leech and Sarah Gustavus-Jones. All made many very useful comments which I have incorporated. To these and not least to my wife Kimberley Reynolds, whose editorial tact and skill are invaluable to me, I owe many thanks.

Introduction

Before beginning a study of Shakespeare's *As You Like It*, it may be useful to be reminded ourselves of the obvious: the work is not a novel or a poem, but a play, and therefore the printed text is incomplete – much remains for the reader to do. For, unlike a novel or a poem, a play is unfinished even when it appears in a bookshop in glossy covers, set in an impressive-looking type-face. Shakespeare may have completed his *As You Like It* in 1599 or thereabouts, or rather he may have completed writing the words he hoped would be spoken by the actors of the Lord Chamberlain's Men, but, once that task was completed, what then existed in manuscript was not *the* play, but a series of complex, indirect instructions as to how *a* play might, eventually, be constructed in performance. Any dramatist's text is incomplete and partial without the added dimension of real or imagined performance. To add that dimension is the task undertaken by those whom I call 'active readers'. It is necessary for such readers to create a 'performance-text' to complete what Shakespeare began, by forging an alliance between intellect and an informed imagination.

Plays become performance not only when they are staged, but when, consciously or unconsciously, readers begin to make choices and take decisions regarding their enactment. Part of this process involves the ability to be *consciously* aware of the nature and range of decisions taken when reading, and constantly to ask whether or not they are appropriate and justified. Whatever eventually is decided, the reader must start by acknowledging that a printed text – even one written by Shakespeare – will need, if it is to come fully alive as drama, a personal text to be added to it. That may seem a daunting or even preposterous suggestion at first – that it could be legitimate or necessary to *add* to what Shakespeare has already made. Surely it is perfect and whole already, and celebrated as such throughout the world by generations of people. But it is not complete and finished, and the active reader does have to *make* the text work.

Perhaps the prospect will appear less intimidating if we begin by remembering that whatever is made of that blueprint originating from the pen of Shakespeare and now in the form of a modern edition of a printed text, it is not going to be destroyed for ever by imaginative actions. One person's thoughts about a play are fugitive, and imaginary reconstructions not indelible; the roof of the Sistine Chapel is not being repainted, nor is Salisbury Cathedral being demolished in order to rebuild it to another design. But part of the task of an active reader of plays is to challenge the apparently final and finished status of what is printed, and the authority it consequently appears to carry with it. The printed word, especially when it appears in book form, is too often accepted as definitive. Students are taught that books contain knowledge, and encouraged to consult them when there is something they need to learn. Very often books seem to lend their owner an air of authority and permanence; indeed, many of us carefully decorate our rooms with them! It would seem a heinous crime to the proud owner of a finely bound, fat volume of prose or verse physically to alter, or change in any way, the words as they appear on the printed page. The perpetrator of such an act might stand accused of literary vandalism. What is printed and bound, the mythology goes, is what the author *meant*; therefore we should not interfere with it in any way at all.

In fact, it is not quite so easy as all that; especially if what is printed is a design for performances, whether on the stage before an audience in a theatre, or in the solitude of the private theatre in the mind. Reading plays, and especially plays by Shakespeare, means that the reader *has* to engage in an active, critical relationship with what is printed, even if s/he is dubious, as some scholars are, that the modern printed text is the full version of Shakespeare's original.

Although dramatists can control what they commit to paper, they cannot control the process in the theatre where what is written is translated into what is performed. There are things that cannot be written down and spoken by actors, which can nevertheless be *shown* in performance to an audience. Equally, what is said by actors speaking the dramatist's text cannot be understood in a vacuum, but only in the context of a given performance. Active readers must attempt to *contextualize* the dramatist's written text in imaginary or recalled performance. The context of that performance will generate its own text, which acts and reacts upon what was originally written by Shakespeare. This performance-text is made up of elements such as the colours used in a setting or costume; what characters wear and how they wear it; their gestural language; the groupings they contrive to make; and the objects or 'props' they use as aids to express personality or to advance the action. This performance-text is also manufactured by those whose task it is to translate dramatic literature into a theatrical event: actors, directors, designers and, not least, audiences.

When reading what is printed to be spoken, active readers must also remember that words themselves are not sovereign in the context of performance. They form part of a larger discourse. To take a simple example: to begin to understand the exchange between two characters as it is printed on the page, it is necessary not only to study the words of the speaker, but also to consider the possible and likely range of responses of the listener. In a performance, listening is also discourse; it is part of the expressive act. To try to be as receptive as possible to the exchange between, say, actors A and B, a reader must *see*, in the theatre of the mind's eye, all aspects of their exchange. It is by balancing the action of the actor who is speaking against the reaction of the actor who is listening and responding that the reader will arrive at an understanding of the complete discourse.

The task of an active reader of plays is to animate the text as it is presented on the page of a modern printed edition, and make it come alive in imaginary production. This is work that should prove exciting, as it requires creativity and intelligence to release the full potential for dramatic expression latent within the printed text of *As You Like It*. But the *reader* has to make it happen. The reader has to make a text that is his or her's and no one else's, and in doing so has to take decisions and accept as legitimate and necessary the accompanying evaluative risks.

Having said that, no reading of a text can be entirely new and original. We are all, to some extent, prisoners of our own literary, critical and theatrical traditions, and thus of culturally determined ways of seeing. Peter Brook, in his now legendary theatre manifesto *The Empty Space*, castigated those whom he called 'deadly spectators'. In particular, he challenged the academic who, he claimed, enjoyed

... routine performances of the classics smiling because nothing has distracted him from trying over and confirming his pet theories to himself, whilst reciting his favourite lines under his breath.[1]

Leaving aside, if possible, whatever constitutes 'routine' performances, and given my impression that most audiences hope not to be denied new readings of old works, there is an underlying assumption in what Brook writes which presumes that the 'ideal', as opposed to the 'deadly', spectator enters the theatre with no preconceptions about what is to be enacted, or the manner in which it is to be communicated in a given performance-space. In other words, the ideal spectator is to be neutral: a blank screen on to which will be projected a fresh and original performance-text. But audiences (and readers) bring to performances, and their private readings of a text, ideas, views, prejudices and opinions derived from their encounters with the processes of education and socialization. What is experienced as the text is inevitably mediated through a veil of expectations, which are conditioned by our experience of life. We look at the world of the play as social animals primed to respond in complex ways, but incapable of being entirely objective or neutral. Judgements about the phenomena being played out on the page/stage are never completely value-free. Even if there existed an audience of people in Britain who had, for example, never read *As You Like It*, it would be almost impossible to produce one that had never heard of Shakespeare. Because the very name 'Shakespeare' is potent, members of an audience necessarily bring with them ideas and expectations about what they are to witness.

Similarly, those whose function it is to enable an audience to make an interpretation of a play (actors, directors and designers) find their problems compounded in respect to Shakespeare. The actress chosen to play Rosalind, for instance, invariably brings to the first rehearsal her half-forgotten and half-suppressed memories of famous occupants of that role, and ideas lingering in her mind from previous productions, witnessed or heard about from others. Performances are historical constructs which include layers of discourse gathered by the oral and written histories of past performances, and the dictates of fashion: it is impossible to avoid echoes from the past in the performance-texts of the present. Although one production stresses its own particular reading, it nevertheless remains a compound, reacting both with and against many others – old and new. For better or worse, readers and audiences come to texts and performances trailing behind them clouds of opinions, memories, prejudices and expectations.

Even if we were able to strip away all the layers which have accrued to a play since it was first performed and somehow find ourselves in the position of the audience at the opening night of *As You Like It*, the work would still not be free from historical associations. The dialogue Shakespeare wrote in 1600 is itself a product of a particular historical moment. *As You Like It* deals with ideas in a way that reflects the thoughts and fashions of its time. It deals, for example, with then-current fashions in what we now loosely term 'pastoral' literature.[2] Pastoral is an ancient literary convention going back as far as the Greek poet Theocritus (c. 316–260 BC), but by the time Shakespeare was beginning to establish himself as a playwright in London, the form had been rediscovered and popularized in English through the publication of works like Spenser's *The Shepherd's Calender* (1579) and Sir Philip Sidney's *Arcadia* (1590). Essentially the convention explored the tension between two very different kinds of world. The first was that of the town (or court), which, although tacitly acknowledged as the home of art and culture (and of the artist himself), was a sophisticated place where corruption and highly artificial behaviour flourished. The other world was that of the countryside. This was idealistically associated with an altogether more simple, direct and honest way of life; a life perceived by its literary creators as essentially innocent and charming. In *As You Like It* Duke Senior extols the virtues of this pastoral world on the first occasion that we see him. He tells us that the Forest of Arden contains 'tongues in trees, books in the running brooks,/Sermons in stones, and good in everything' (II.1.16–17). All very different from the court, that place disparagingly referred to by the Duke as the world of 'painted pomp'. But as the action of *As You Like It* reveals, despite his evident infatuation with an ideal, the Duke is not slow to return to the reality of the despised court when a realistic opportunity presents itself. Shakespeare himself was familiar with both town and country life, and knew well that the literary pastoral world, with its innocent rustics, and charming and beautiful shepherds and shepherdesses, was far removed from the real life of country people. Nevertheless he obviously recognized the topical uses to which the form could be put, and perhaps also the human need for pastoral 'escapist' literature.

The result of this concern with topical issues is an enjoyable tension between aspects of *As You Like It* that mirror that pastoral convention (the action is full of improbabilities, and peopled by aristocrats thinly disguised as country people) and those that show Shakespeare's direct knowledge of real country life. He invited his sophisticated and fundamentally urban audience to see the Forest of Arden through a double focus. One lens shows a story that is highly artificial, expressed in a stylized way, full of fairy-tale characters who instantly fall in love and manage, apparently effortlessly, to escape any significant threats to their happiness. The other lens reveals the closely observed, soil-conscious world of Corin and Silvius, Audrey and Phebe, who are themselves none the less transformed into pastoral types, amusing in their simplicity. They exist in the play as both genuine rustics and diverting parodies of the modes of pastoral love.

Throughout this book, but particularly in the commentary that follows in the next chapter, I deal more specifically with some of the other literary concerns of *As You Like It*. However, great plays of the past (and all great works of literature) continue to have a lively existence in the present because they contain ideas that transcend their immediate historical context. It is what Jonathan Miller has called the 'afterlife' of plays that primarily interested me in writing this book. With this in mind, I have constructed three imaginary directors, all of whom manufacture a potential performance-text of *As You Like It* in their own terms. Although one cannot and should not ignore the fact that a 400-year-old play reflects the thought of its time, in performance it also reflects the thoughts of its actors, director and audience. Looking at the events of the past from the perspective of the present tells us almost as much about ourselves as it does about history. A play has an existence that is, to an extent, creatively independent of its original conditions of production. Knowledge of late-Elizabethan contemporary thought and literary conventions may well open up a text of that period to the scholarly reader and reveal meanings previously obscured by ignorance. However, a theatrically successful parody of a sixteenth-century literary convention cannot be made for a twentieth-century audience or readership largely ignorant of it. For me, therefore, the real excitement in reading plays theatrically comes not only from knowledge gained through a process of literary archaeology, but also from using the informed imagination to probe the 'possibility of unforeseen meanings'.[3]

That can seem daunting – how, from all the many texts generated over the past four hundred years, can one person hope to make a meaningful 'unforeseen' reading of *As You Like It*? In the second, third and fourth chapters I attempt to illustrate that this process of claiming a text as your own is both possible and inevitable. Three imaginary directors demonstrate specific lines of dramatic interpretation, emanating from three very different critical and theatrical perspectives. They all use identical material as their starting point – the modern Penguin text of *As You Like It* (edited by H. J. Oliver) – but the significance each attributes to it, and the subsequent presentational strategies they adopt, differ widely. If they were ever to meet they would certainly disagree violently on what certain aspects of the play mean; but each would, I hope, be able to argue, on the basis of textual evidence, for the validity of his or her position.

I am interested in good arguments and good theatre. I hope the reader will agree, whether siding with one or none of them, that their arguments, although conflicting and perhaps sometimes extreme, all have some validity and strength. Remember in approaching the text of this play as active readers that although no master-text exists for a definitive reading of *As You Like It* an alliance of the intellect and the theatrical imagination is required to animate it successfully, either in reality or in the theatre of the mind's eye. All potential interpretations of a text are *not* all equally valid. If the reader decides to take up a critical position on this text, or any other, that cannot be defended by referring directly to what is printed for actors to speak, s/he will be in difficulty – perhaps with audiences, certainly with critics and examiners!

Remember too when watching performances in the theatre, or when recommended to read a particular critic, that the aim of most criticism (and of most performances) is to try to convince you to see the text from one particular point of view, often to the exclusion of others. I hope the very different, but none the less valid, perspectives on *As You Like It* articulated by the three hypothetical directors will help create a balanced view of this complex play, and serve as the starting point for alternative readings.

In order that this book does not, like the play itself, become an entire fiction, in addition to the opening commentary I have included an extract from a real performance-text of *As You Like It* created by the Royal Shakespeare Company working with the director Terry Hands.

1. A Dramatic Commentary

What follows is not a detailed scene-by-scene analysis of the play. I have simply discussed the action sequentially and drawn the attention of the reader to points in the text that I find particularly interesting or significant. Inevitably some incidents in the action are given greater attention than others; this indicates *my* interests and preoccupations and not necessarily those of Shakespeare.

Act I Scene 1

Beginnings are perhaps the most difficult task confronting any writer. If the reader is put off at the outset, it is unlikely that what follows will receive much attention. The same is true, although perhaps more so, in the theatre. There, when the lights in the auditorium dim, the audience's intense focus on the stage can soon be dissipated and lost if the clues encoded in the printed page have not been effectively deciphered and translated by the performers into effective theatre language. At the opening of the performance we are usually introduced to some of the major characters and themes, which the subsequent action will explore. It is a time when the audience first gets an opportunity to 'read' the theatrical designer's text, which, together with the actors, sets up a location and, more importantly, a mood and atmosphere for the play.

The location of the opening scene of *As You Like It* is the orchard attached to the house of Orlando's brother Oliver. An orchard is a place associated with fecundity – with growth and fruitfulness. But in order for nature to be productive it needs to be tended and nourished. Nature requires nurture in order to grow and thrive. The setting thus works as a background metaphor for the life of the young protagonist who first appears there. The action begins with the entrance into the orchard of two men – Orlando and Adam. They are in marked contrast to each other: one is near the end of his life, the other on the threshold of independence and maturity; one is physically weak, the other healthy and strong. Their costumes present a designer with an opportunity of indicating their social status; both appear to be rustics, simple country men, who are servants rather than masters. However there is a contrast between the visual impression given by the two actors and that conveyed by their spoken text. Orlando speaks in far from impoverished language about the recent past. From what he says it is clear that he and Adam are in the middle of a conversation, and that an established relationship of friendship and intimacy exists between them. Through their dialogue the audience learns of a conflict. Orlando tells of the unnatural behaviour of his older brother, who, despite being charged by their father to 'breed me well', neglects the husbandry necessary if Orlando's natural potential is to flourish in the world. This then is the first news of dislocation: an older brother is not conforming to the unwritten rules of conduct in society.

After hearing a story about the conduct of an elder brother and, as yet, having no way of knowing whether or not the story is correct, the audience sees the brother himself enter the stage. Adam identifies him. During the following exchange between Oliver and Orlando, Adam becomes a silent but expressive witness. Again, costume is potentially important in distinguishing between the material status of the two brothers. Oliver could be dressed to emphasize his superior financial and social position. His tone is aggressive, more reminiscent of a master/servant relationship than that of brother to brother. This treatment of his young sibling invites comparison with the genuine master/servant relationship (Orlando and Adam), which relies on mutual trust and affection, and that of Oliver and Adam, in which the servant is treated with ill-disguised contempt. The verbal confrontation between Orlando and Oliver soon escalates into a physical struggle. Orlando's grappling with his brother provides a potent image of dislocation, and also prefigures both the wrestling match and the subsequent struggle of right versus might, which the play chronicles. Adam steps between the two brothers and prevents further escalation of the trouble.

Oliver's behaviour, although within the letter of the law, is being made to be seen as outside the spirit of it. Adam and Orlando have enacted a text that informs the audience that something is wrong, but it has not always been so. There has been a time in the past – a golden age – which is lost (but Adam can recall it), and what is lost may perhaps be regained.

After the exit of Adam and Orlando, Oliver is left alone on stage just long enough to confirm the impression that he is a villain. The arrival and subsequent exchange with Charles the wrestler creates an opportunity for stressing another dramatic contrast. Charles should be shown as a physically powerful man, for he is, as it were, an emblem of the power entrusted to Oliver by his father, but turned to improper use. In the exchange between the two, the audience learns some important information and also hears, for the first time, the name of Rosalind. The Forest of Arden is mentioned and a tale told that has a distinct parallel with what the audience have just seen and heard. They learn now not of an older brother abusing his privileges of birth, but of a younger brother who has usurped the rights of an elder; in both cases the legitimate moral order is turned on its head. But all the relationships to which the scene introduces us are not unnatural. Adam and Orlando are almost like father and son, while Charles describes Rosalind and Celia as cousins who are manifestly an example of the natural and right bond of blood: 'never two ladies loved as they do'. Oliver lies to Charles, inciting him not only to take on Orlando as a challenger, but to do his worst against him. This is just one of many deceptions practised in the course of the play. With the departure of the wrestler, Oliver is again alone. He continues his villainy and, with unconscious irony, further distances himself from his brother by listing all the latter's positive qualities: 'learned', 'noble', 'gentle', one who, as he puts it, is 'in the heart of the world'.

Thus in this exposition Shakespeare sets a blood relationship, which ought naturally to be harmonious but is in fact at odds, against one with no ties of blood, but where there is an expression of a natural bond of sympathy and feeling. We have also heard of another set of brothers (Duke Frederick and Duke Senior) who have disrupted the natural order, and of a pair of cousins (Celia and Rosalind), who are the embodiment of what that order *should* be.

Act I Scene 2

Recognizing how Shakespeare organizes incidents and events is a very important part of trying to understand the way in which meaning is manufactured in performance.[4] The order in which the audience sees the action unfolding is carefully contrived: certain events are scenically juxtaposed in order to make dramatic effects and meaning. Placing sequentially two contrasting images, or series of images, invites comparison. Thus at the beginning of scene 2 we are invited to compare and contrast the relationships of two couples, both united by ties of blood. In scene 1 two brothers are disunited and fractious; in scene 2 two cousins are united and harmonious. The closeness of Celia and Rosalind is immediately indicated by the opening spoken text: Celia addresses Rosalind as her 'coz' and uses a familiar term of endearment, 'sweet', which is reciprocated by Rosalind's '*Dear* Celia' (my emphasis). This is in contrast to the abrupt and formal address with which Oliver greets Orlando: 'Now, sir, what make you here?'

The closeness of the women and the separateness of the men can also be emphasized by the gestures of the actors playing them. In the interaction between Celia and Rosalind it is Celia who is the optimist; she urges Rosalind to put the past behind her. The cousins then begin a verbal game that is intricate and verbally prefigures the wrestling match we are soon to witness. But the women's game is a harmless pastime that defuses aggression.

During this combat the audience first see Touchstone. Celia identifies him in terms of familiarity, adding sufficient indications so that we can recognize his role in the court is a special one: he is a fool, a professional jester, and thus one who is marginal in this society. Touchstone's position makes it possible for him to speak aloud what many think only in private. He fulfils the role of fool to the court of Duke Frederick, but he is also cast in the role of loyal friend to Celia and Rosalind. Helen Gardner has said of him:

The essence of clowning is adaptability and improvization. The clown is never baffled and is marked by his ability to place himself at once in rapport with his audience, to be all things to all men, to play the part which is required at the moment. Touchstone sustains many different roles. After hearing Silvius's lament and Rosalind's echo of it, he becomes the maudlin lover of Jane Smile; with the simple shepherd Corin he becomes a cynical and worldly wiseman of the court; with Jacques he is a melancholy moralist, musing on the power of time and the decay of all things; with the Pages he acts the lordly amateur of the arts, patronizing the musicians.[5]

In this, the first sighting of him by the audience, he informs them of the cold climate of this court, where to speak out is a hazard:

CELIA ... you'll be whipped for taxation one of these days.
TOUCHSTONE The more pity that fools may not speak wisely what wise men do foolishly.
CELIA By my troth, thou sayest true ...

(I.2.80–84)

Touchstone has referred to Rosalind's father, to whom it is dangerous to allude in public. The fact that he does so, and that Celia not only does not try to stop him but actually agrees with what he says, creates an immediate sense of conspiracy between the three. It prepares us for their flight, and simultaneously encourages belief in the shared perception of the truth which unites them. That truth is that so-called wise men (i.e. Duke Frederick) are behaving foolishly.

The entrance of Le Beau adds further to the impression that all is far from well at the court of Duke Frederick. As well as introducing the wrestling, his part offers an opportunity for an actor to demonstrate, both through costume and gesture, the kind of courtier who flourishes in this environment; a type in contrast to those soon to be seen around the court of Duke Senior in the Forest of Arden. Le Beau informs the audience of the nature of this 'sport', which seems unsavoury if not actually decadent. He has just witnessed three sons of an old man defeated and left with 'little hope of life'. It is Touchstone who reminds the audience, should they need reminding, that this is no ordinary wholesome sport: 'It is the first time that ever I heard breaking of ribs was sport for ladies' (I.2.128–9).

The entrance of Duke Frederick, his court and Charles and Orlando makes the stage crowded for the first time in the action. In addition to the seven named characters on stage, there are assorted lords and attendants. The latter are important even though they have no words (or very few) to speak. Like Le Beau, at this time, their dramatic function is to indicate what kind of a court this is. A director, and an active reader, has to decide what to do with them. Do they indicate the presence of factions? Do some of them apparently disapprove of the spectacle of the public wrestling (remember that we are told that many men from the court have flocked to join the exiled Duke Senior); do others vociferously support it? The courtiers provide an audience for the wrestling match itself, and collectively create an appropriate atmosphere for it. Presumably they are all male, thus emphasizing the isolation of Rosalind and Celia in this environment.

The staging of the bout is difficult to dramatize convincingly. But it should, I suggest, be treated seriously and not, as it sometimes is, as a joke. Charles does not have to be a super-heavyweight, but he must be demonstrably the more powerful of the two. It is natural ability and acquired skill which defeat him, not superior strength.

The age of the challenger is stressed a good deal. Celia says he's too young to fight and Rosalind addresses him as 'young man'. Both women entreat Orlando to avoid the conflict. But fight he does – and wins! His victory is one example of many in the play of the deceptive nature of external appearances: they prove to be shallow and unreliable guides to the inner and true state (and status) of a person.

When the fight is over, instead of the customary and merited award, Orlando receives a rebuff. Duke Frederick's reaction to learning Orlando's name and parentage indicates a link between his own behaviour and that of Orlando's brother Oliver. Both are dominated by their hatred for individuals whom others admire: 'The world esteemed thy father honourable,/But I did

find him still mine enemy' (I.2.213–14). The 'I' isolates Duke
Frederick from the rest of the world. It is *his* judgement that is
maverick and out of harmony with 'all the world'. That same
world of public opinion had also acclaimed Orlando. Thus it is
clear that both Duke Frederick and Oliver are the outsiders; it is
their behaviour rather than that of the exiled Duke or of Orlando
that is aberrant. They have deviated from the norm. The important fact is the affirmation that a norm does exist, and
indications are already being laid that one of the play's concerns
is to identify this golden mean and regain it. These values,
though driven out of the court, have not been lost altogether; it
soon becomes apparent that they are sheltering in the Forest of
Arden.

The wrestling match, then, is a metaphor for the dislocation
of those in power. But it is also a metaphor for falling in love.
Through the struggle, Rosalind identifies herself with Orlando,
and both bring the optimism of love into what is otherwise a
dark scene of threats and violence. The suddenness with which
love enters the hearts of the characters is typical of Shakespearian comedy. What is later said of Celia and Oliver could
equally well have been said of Rosalind and Orlando: '. . . no
sooner looked but they loved'. This suddenness mirrors the
sudden movement in which Duke Frederick turns away from
the victory of Orlando. In this scene, and especially in the images
and events surrounding the wrestling match, the behaviour of
men and women is continually shown to be subject to powerful
forces which they imperfectly control and which they cannot
fully understand. Just as the natural order is overthrown by
usurpers and bad guardians, causing a new but unstable state of
political affairs, so the lovers are shown to be toppled. You fall
in love; being in that state entails – like falling – loss of control,
a feeling of disorientation and surrender of self.

Act I Scene 3

After all the action of scene 2 the next scene is much calmer and
more reflective. This is deliberate and theatrically appropriate,
for the audience cannot sustain that level of intensity; there is

need for relaxation, reflection and, of course, entertainment. The third scene offers further confirmation of the friendship and love that exists between the two young women as Celia tries to cheer and comfort her friend. She recalls the wrestling, thereby focusing attention on the fact that Rosalind has fallen in love with Orlando. She also reminds the audience and Rosalind that he is the son of old Sir Rowland. This is important because Rosalind gives this as one of the reasons for her immediate attraction to Orlando: 'The Duke my father loved his father dearly' (I.3.29). But as the wise Celia points out, reason is not enough; reason indeed gets corrupted. You cannot use a rational argument to explain love. As we have seen, love, unlike blood, cannot be inherited. If such feeling could be transmitted then, as Celia says, Rosalind should indeed love Orlando because her father loved his father, but equally Celia should '. . . hate him, for my father hated his father dearly; yet I hate not Orlando' (I.3.31–3).

The entrance of Duke Frederick, possessed by anger, serves paradoxically to bind rather than to part the two young women. Ultimately the tie of love proves stronger than that of duty. His wrath serves to unite not only Celia and Rosalind, but also eventually, Orlando and Rosalind: both are to be banished on pain of death. Again reason is inadequate in this situation. Rosalind uses it to no avail in her plea 'Treason is not inherited' (I.3.59). Duke Frederick is beyond the power of true reason, and is subject to his own brand of perverse paranoid logic. He not only turns against Rosalind but against his own daughter, twice calling her 'fool'. (We may well remember that Touchstone has told us that in this world 'fools' see and speak the truth.) This storm of anger blows the two together and, at Celia's prompting, they begin to conspire how to leave. The fact that they decide to adopt disguises is symbolic of the fact that they were leaving behind their old selves in the old world. The people they were there will not serve in the new and different world that awaits them in the Forest of Arden.

Act II Scene 1

This scene opens by introducing us to that other world. There is preserved a set of values different from those which now prevail at Duke Frederick's court. This is the court in exile.

The first vision of the courtiers is obviously important. The stage directions say that they are dressed 'like foresters'. However you decide visually to interpret that note, their garments should be in contrast to the clothes deemed appropriate at Frederick's court. Perhaps they should be simple and unostentatious, in common with the life-style of their wearers.

The first person to speak, who the audience later learns is the banished Duke Senior (Rosalind's father), immediately refers to that world which has occupied the preceding scenes of the play. He emphasizes the view that it is an unnatural place; a world of 'painted pomp', of disguise and deception, and full of envy. By contrast, here in the forest – the natural world – men are daily reminded of the more fundamental and basic realities of the human condition; which underlie *all* behaviour, however civilized or sophisticated. By implication the court of Duke Frederick has moved too far away from what is natural and basic: they have forgotten who they really are, or rather *what* they are. Duke Senior may be a Duke, but he is like all other men in this cold climate. His rank cannot protect him from the cold: 'This is no flattery; these are counsellors/That feelingly persuade me what I am' (II.1.10–11).

In this scene we are introduced, for the first time, to another of the major characters in the play: Jaques. Although we do not see him, we hear of his reaction to the hunting of the deer and are twice told that he is melancholy. The talk of hunting is the bridge which takes us on to the next scene.

Act II Scene 2

We are once more back in the court, and the entrance of Duke Frederick with his accompanying lords is set against the images of his brother and his followers in the preceding scene. They literally follow one another on to and off stage. If any doubt has previously existed, it is now clear that Duke Frederick's is an unnatural world. The fact is driven home by the dialogue, which is a perverted echo of that in II.1 where Duke Senior and his followers are speaking of hunting. So too does his brother – but he speaks of a man hunt.

Act II Scene 3

Still in the court, the audience is confronted with the spectacle of two of the hunted: Adam and Orlando. This scene is a transition between the two worlds: Adam and Orlando have not yet left the court but they are, like Rosalind and Celia before them, preparing to do so. In their exchange we learn more of the topsy-turvy world of Duke Frederick's court, where '. . . what is comely/Envenoms him that bears it!' (II.3.14–15). This is an inversion of what ought to happen, just as the relationship between Orlando and Adam is backwards: it is Adam, the old man with no breeding or position, who is helping his younger master. An escape from the corrupt court, and the wrath of Oliver, is made possible because of Adam. He grew up in a world now very distant from that experienced by young Orlando. By comparison to the present it seemed a 'golden world'. In that past time it seems men behaved responsibly and with compassion. Unlike Duke Frederick and Oliver they had due regard for the rights of others and the obligations of power. Indeed, thanks to the behaviour of Sir Rowland de Boys towards his servant Adam, he provides not only for the servant but also, unknowingly, for the son. You could argue that had it not been for the original act of goodness and respect for the rights of others, which led to this subsequent and unforeseen working out in the world, the values from which it derived (those of the antique world) would never have been regained. The notion of the myth of an older, better world, which is emphasized here, is a dominant theme of the play and explains much of what follows.

Act II Scene 4

At the beginning of Act II Rosalind's father detailed some of the delights of the pastoral life. However, as the director of the Romantic text will make clear, the countryside of Arden sometimes looks very different to its permanent residents than it does to those whose stay is temporary and for whom it is a 'holiday world' rather than a home. At the beginning of this scene – the first time we see Rosalind and Celia in their disguises – the forest looks to them a distinctly unpromising place. In many performances of the play I have heard the actress playing Rosalind place stress on the second word of her line and turn it into a question: 'Well, *this* is the Forest of Arden?' Instead of any immediate sense of relief at their escape from the court, all three – Rosalind, Celia and especially Touchstone – seem preoccupied and tired. Touchstone, far from feeling that he is now on holiday, states quite baldly that, in his view, they were better off at home.

Not for the last time in the Forest of Arden Touchstone performs the role suggested by his name: he reminds the other characters, and the audience, of the sometimes unpleasant nature of reality. For, as Rosalind has remarked, 'this is the Forest of Arden' and therefore, supposedly, a pastoral world – a demi-paradise, if the poets are to be believed. But Shakespeare is no ordinary poet and, in the expression of his heartfelt desire to be at home, he has Touchstone sum up the reaction of all the newly arrived visitors to the forest. What Touchstone does is to remind us that this place is very different from the world of the countryside created in more traditional Elizabethan pastoral literature. Shakespeare's Arden is based on the observation of the realities of country life. Of course, within that world some of the conventions of pastoral still apply; disguised aristocrats do fall hopelessly in love, and the miraculous is just around the next bush. But Touchstone (and Jaques) always manage to pull the audience back from an overly sentimental attachment to the romantic idealization of life, which is open to those who tend to focus exclusively on what happens to Rosalind and Orlando. These two *do* fall hopelessly in love in the approved fashion of pastoral romance, but the affair of Touchstone and Audrey mocks that convention and reminds us all of the reality of desire and lust that underlies literary idealizations of the state of 'being in love'.

Shakespeare further deflates the conventional assumptions about the pastoral or holiday world by his presentation of two of its permanent residents: Corin and Silvius. If this place is paradise, why are these two anything but happy? The first is in an agony of unrequited love. The second has a master who treats him almost as badly as Oliver did Orlando: 'My master is of churlish disposition,/And little recks to find the way to heaven/By doing deeds of hospitality' (II.4.77–9).

This scene is the first test for Rosalind's male disguise as Ganymede. Fortunately it seems to work, as Corin confirms:

ROSALIND Peace, I say. Good even to you, friend.
CORIN And to you, gentle sir . . .

(II.4.66–7)

The disguise may hide Rosalind's sex, but her voice and speech cannot disguise her class. Corin recognizes (as does Orlando later) that she is 'gentle', that is, of gentle birth.

Although the pastoral world is normally associated with romance, escapism and dreams come true, Rosalind and Celia need a very down-to-earth commodity in order to sustain themselves there: money. They are able (and apparently it is necessary) to 'buy entertainment', 'cottage', 'pasture' and 'flock', and to 'mend' (improve) Corin's wages. Thus this world of Arden is more like the world of the court than it may at first have appeared. People are unhappy within it; there are masters who abuse their servants; and those of high birth, despite their disguises, have the means, and the need, to employ servants.

Act II Scene 5

The focus of the play now turns away from the permanent residents to the temporary inhabitants of Arden. Unlike Silvius and Corin, these exiles seem unconcerned with difficulties and practicalities and, as if to emphasize this, the action begins with a song. Amiens's lyric, and in particular the reference 'Here shall he see/No enemy/But winter and rough weather' (II.5.6–8), reminds the audience of Duke Senior's speech about why he finds his holiday world so admirable:

> ... the icy fang
> And churlish chiding of the winter's wind,
> Which when it bites and blows upon my body
> Even till I shrink with cold, I smile and say
> 'This is no flattery; these are counsellors
> That feelingly persuade me what I am'
>
> (II.1.6–11)

Whilst listening to the first verse of Amiens's song, the audience have time to observe the character of Jaques and note his response to the music. His presence is registered by Amiens, who teases him about his melancholy disposition. Here then is another example that in this supposed pastoral or holiday world everyone does not subscribe to the optimism of Amiens's lyrics, or to the Duke's celebration of the natural world. A contemporary Elizabethan (Sir Thomas Overbury) described the conventional melancholy man:

a strayer from the drove ... His imagination is never idle, it keeps his mind in a continual motion, as the poise of a clock; he winds up thoughts often, and as often unwinds them ... He'll seldom be found without the shades of some grove, in whose bottom a river dwells ... He thinks business, but never does any; he is all contemplation, no action ...

It is a description that seems to fit Jaques.

Act II Scene 6

As in II.4, we see the entry of travellers. They too are tired. Adam, like Celia, 'can go no further', and their environment appears to be uninviting and hostile. Orlando describes it as 'uncouth'; a 'desert' in which the air is 'bleak', and Adam very much in need of 'shelter'. Their arrival in Arden does not suggest an auspicious beginning to their new life. It seems they have fled the perils of the 'civilized' world only to encounter those of the natural one.

Act II Scene 7

The audience now gets its first opportunity to observe the whole of the court in exile. Many directors pick up on the remark of Charles the wrestler, in I.1., when he tells Oliver that the exile of Duke Senior is acting as a magnet: '. . . they say many young gentlemen flock to him every day' (I.1.110–111). The present scene provides an opportunity to show characters previously seen at court (perhaps some of those who visibly expressed disquiet at the wrestling match) now happily settled in the forest. I have seen a production in which Charles himself has followed on, now to live a more peaceful, less stressful existence.[6]

When Jaques enters and tells of his meeting with Touchstone (a meeting which has certainly animated him) we have a report of the first contact between the established settlers and the new arrivals. The reported contact is rapidly replaced by the reality of Orlando's entrance. This first encounter is a confrontation: he bursts upon the scene to the surprise of the exiled courtiers and, to his amazement – for he thought this place a 'barren desert' – he finds a banquet spread before him. This display of plenty, so much in contrast to his and Adam's need, provokes him to demand: 'Forbear, and eat no more.' It is Jaques who defuses the tension by his failure to take seriously the physical armed threat apparently posed by the young intruder. The Duke and Jaques passify Orlando and enable him to see something else about this deceptive place:

ORLANDO Speak you so gently? Pardon me, I pray you.
  I thought that all things had been savage here. . .

(II.7.107–8)

From this encounter the audience learns that the court of Duke Senior is very unlike that of his younger brother Duke Frederick. Here in the forest these men preserve a culture that values acts of charity, that prizes compassion and friendship. They may well have seen better days in material terms, but spiritually they are wealthy. Like the behaviour of old Sir Rowland towards his servant Adam, the response to Orlando's need is one founded in the ordered and virtuous values of the past.

There are, in a sense, two songs in this scene. The first is spoken – Jaques's 'aria' on the seven ages of man (which will be commented on in the Romantic text) – while the second is sung by Amiens. They share beautiful language, rich in imagery, and move their listeners. More importantly, both are only partially true. Although what Jaques says is, in a literal sense, true enough – we do pass from cradle to grave through distinct and recognizable stages – yet something crucial is surely missing from his philosophy: as the director of the Romantic text remarks, it is all very well to describe the journey; the point is whether or not you choose to attach any significance to it. The arrival of Orlando carrying Adam demonstrates that the journey can be *given* significance by the charitable actions of the travellers themselves. So too, in Amiens's song, it may be true to say that '*most* friendship is feigning, *most* loving mere folly' (my italics), but there are – as evidenced by Orlando, Adam, Rosalind and Celia – joyous exceptions, offering hope for a positive response to the world.

Act III Scene 1

In many ways the previous scene is one of the most idyllic in the whole play. In it people behave well towards one another; we can see, and we are meant to see, a dim reflection of that golden world now lost but never completely forgotten, with which these people are able to remain in touch. Our shock then is great when we next are forced to move out of Arcadia and back into the court of Duke Frederick. It is the last time we shall see him. Frederick's meeting with Oliver casts Orlando's brother in the role of huntsman. It is, of course, ironic and true to the nature of this place that the Duke suspects Oliver of conniving in his brother's disappearance. He even suspects him of hiding Orlando!

Act III Scene 2

Shakespeare is quick to establish that we are back in the forest. As if to emphasize the difference between the forest and the court we have just left, he presents Orlando, now unwittingly the object of a hunt, preoccupied with things other than the jealousy and hatred that obsess both his brother and Duke Frederick: he is in love. Orlando is engaged in the delightfully foolish game of pinning up his poetry as a public declaration of his love for Rosalind. It is a kind of Elizabethan graffiti that we do not find offensive. The discovery of his verses is delayed by the entrance of Corin and Touchstone.

In everything he says Touchstone avoids sentimentality. The potential risk of slipping into whimsy by concentrating for too long on the lovers (for, like drunks, lovers are only really interesting to each other) is avoided by the contrast this meeting of Touchstone and Corin presents. Being in love is a state the Elizabethans associated with sentiments about the pastoral life; but, in response to Corin's question, 'And how like you this shepherd's life . . .?', Touchstone, far from eulogizing it, satirizes the sort of sophistication with which some of Shakespeare's own contemporaries argued in favour of the pastoral idea. None the less, there are important values present in the country that are conspicuously lacking in the city. Although Touchstone displays a use of language that calls on skills learnt at court (perhaps from listening to the verbal exchanges of Celia and Rosalind), his flourishes are met with a directness and simplicity that is a match for his more florid style. In the exchange between the man of the city and the man of the country, it is the countryman who comes off best. Touchstone displays the city dweller's superiority towards Corin, as later he does towards William. In doing so, however, he unintentionally demonstrates how superficial courtly attitudes can be. In this scene, the fool seems to be something of a bully; and if he deflates the pastoral idea, he certainly does not lead us to decry the naturalness of the shepherd.

The entrance of Rosalind shifts the focus back to love. When she reads out the first of Orlando's poems, Touchstone is still in the role of arbiter of what is acceptable to persons from the court. He satirizes the poor verse unmercifully, undercutting the language of love. When Celia enters she contributes to this very public poetry reading, but she, unlike Rosalind (or Touchstone), is aware of the identity of the author. Interestingly, the opening lines of verse spoken by Celia do seem to recall the more polished poetry of Jaques and Amiens, in particular the seven ages of man speech and the song with the verse 'Most friendship is feigning, most loving mere folly.' But the melancholia of both has been rejected by Orlando:

> Some, how brief the life of man
>   Runs his erring pilgrimage,
> That the stretching of a span
>   Buckles in his sum of age;
> Some, of violated vows
>   'Twixt the souls of friend and friend;
>   (III.2.125–30)

In spite of their sentiments, even Rosalind's patience expires before Celia has finished reading. Before revealing the secret of its authorship Celia dismisses Touchstone, for this is no time for mocking. Celia is not above teasing her friend in a way that must surely be familiar to almost anybody who has experienced the delights and perils of adolescent love. When finally she reveals the identity of the poor poet, Rosalind's first thought is how to get rid of her disguise!

The entrance of Orlando and Jaques causes mounting excitement in the cousins as they, like children playing a party game, 'slink by' and 'note him'. What they witness is another kind of wrestling match, where once again Orlando is the victor. His optimism and faith in the power of his own love easily overcome the temptation to join Jaques in railing against the world. Orlando has opted in; Jaques has opted out. Jaques's cynical world-weariness has no place here; he is dismissed by Orlando, condemned as a fool. A harsh judgement perhaps, but Jaques certainly misjudges the situation and the humour of the young man: a man in love welcomes the departure of melancholy.

When Jaques has gone, and Orlando is left alone on stage to be joined by Celia and Rosalind, Rosalind's disguise faces its biggest test yet: will Orlando recognize the woman with whom he says he is in love? Certainly there is no indication at the beginning of their encounter that he does. What soon develops between them is yet another verbal game, in which Rosalind is the dominant partner, leading the somewhat dazed Orlando through a maze of rhetorical tricks on the subject of time. As she is speaking he has time to observe her and there is just a hint of suspicion in his voice when he asks 'Where dwell you, pretty youth?' If the actor puts the stress on the first word in the line, the effect is to make it clear that Orlando is surprised and a little confused at such wit issuing from the brother of a shepherdess. Rosalind's answer obviously fails to satisfy him completely, and again he asks 'Are you *native* of this place?' (my emphasis). Fortunately for Rosalind, it is apparently her accent, rather than her gender, that has confused her lover, and she is able quickly to devise a rather limp explanation by inventing an 'old religious uncle'. In their subsequent exchange Rosalind teases Orlando with the daring suggestion – daring at least as far as she and the silent but expressive figure of Celia is concerned – of having him pretend that Ganymede is in fact his own love, Rosalind.

Act III Scene 3

This scene serves as a marvellous contrast to the last. Now, instead of a romantic adventure between two delightful young people, we see another very different couple. Touchstone and Audrey are more interested in the immediate gratification of their desires than they are in playing courtship games. Touchstone seems to want to consummate the relationship almost before it has begun. His relationship with this rather coarse country girl calls into question the whole notion that relationships between men and women can be romantic. He wishes the gods had made Audrey 'poetical' (i.e. more like the shepherdesses of pastoral fiction), but Audrey does not even profess to know what 'poetical' is. She asks if it means honest and true. 'No, truly [says Touchstone]: for the truest poetry is the most feigning [here punning on the two meanings of the word]; and lovers are given to poetry; and what they swear in poetry may be said as lovers they do feign' (III.3.17–19). This exchange touches on Elizabethan controversies about whether or not poets were liars, especially the courtly poets who specialized in romantic poems. It also calls into question the sincerity of Phebe and Orlando, those lovers who declare themselves in poetry. In case this does not sufficiently undermine the concept of love, Touchstone's further exchange with Audrey is altogether anti-romantic: he calls her a foul slut and praises the gods for her foulness. He then proceeds to pun on the word horn, a comic device that, judging by how frequently Shakespeare uses it, never failed to delight Elizabethan audiences whose ears flapped for sexual innuendoes. Yet this wit is lost on Audrey, as his earlier arguments were wasted on Corin; language is used for no real purpose, words are futile.

Act III Scene 4

In the last few scenes of this play there are frequent reminders that the world is like 'a wide and universal theatre', and that men and women are 'merely players'. In real life we all assume roles: in writing this I am taking the role of author; you, in reading it, assume the role of reader; but we have both professional roles and domestic ones. Thus a policeman 'on duty' has a role to play which differs from the one he occupies as a son, a father, a brother and so on. Those readers who have studied drama will know that by simulating the taking-on of a new role it is often possible to add to the knowledge and understanding of a character. Not only does an actor adopt a role when s/he undertakes to play, say, Rosalind or Jaques, but in turn that character adopts one or more roles, according to circumstance.

Rosalind is a good example of someone who learns through adopting a role. One of her main roles is that of Ganymede. In the Forest of Arden, although her male disguise has, in some respects, liberated her from the social constraints attached to single women, she also can feel trapped in her role. For example in the preceding scene, in which the identity of the poet is revealed by Celia to be her lover, she immediately wishes to assume her old, familiar role of a woman. Once she decides to maintain her disguise she has to create a personality to fit. Thus when anticipating her first meeting with Orlando as Ganymede, she determines to 'speak to him like a saucy lacky, and under that habit play the knave with him' (III.2.287–8). Her role even involves creating a history for her character: Ganymede has an old religious uncle who brought him up and warned him against courtship. Disguise – even lying – do have both their rewards and penalties for Rosalind. They enable her to state obliquely her true feelings for Orlando, but her role as a sort of androgynous Rosalind-substitute does not work entirely to her advantage. When, as in this scene, Orlando is late, Rosalind is almost in tears. Celia, although she plays the role of a shepherdess, none the less retains her feminine character throughout, and has to remind Rosalind that she is acting out of character, observing that 'tears do not become a man'. For Rosalind, Orlando's non-arrival is emotionally painful; but for Orlando the whole business is *just* a game. This whole concept of role-playing is reinforced at the end of the scene when Corin comes on to urge the cousins to see 'a pageant truly played', and Rosalind's distress is soon forgotten in her desire not only to observe Phebe and Silvius, but also to 'prove a busy actor in their play' (III.4.55).

Act III Scene 5

In this scene we have a remarkable dramatic encounter. In Rosalind we have (if we recall the original conditions of performance for *As You Like It*) a boy playing the part of a girl, disguised as a boy. But in the exchange we now witness we see Phebe, played originally by a boy actor, falling in love with another boy actor playing a girl disguised as a boy!

Of course Phebe and Silvius ought, given the Elizabethan conventions of pastoral (shepherds and shepherdesses were supposed to live in harmony), to be ideally suited to each other, but their dislocation is yet another example of the reality of Shakespeare's forest as opposed to the artificiality of the more traditional version of pastoral life. Phebe and Silvius should, I suggest, be played by actors who look as much like Rosalind and Orlando as possible, for what Shakespeare is doing is showing the audience that it is the thinnest of lines that separates one couple's happiness from another's sadness. Love involves suffering as well as exultation: the situation of Rosalind and Orlando could, he seems to suggest, so easily be that of Phebe and Silvius. Love is not always instantly reciprocated. To be young and open to love is also to risk being open to rejection. The message, if there is one, is to approach love with eyes open to the possibility that things in real life may not turn out as they do in fairy-tale romances.

Act IV Scene 1

The attempt by Jaques to become 'better acquainted' with Rosalind fails for the same reason that he has previously failed to find favour with Orlando: the youthful enthusiasm of the young lovers leaves no room for the melancholic reflections of old age. Perhaps we should take seriously Phebe's passing remark that Jaques is an 'old gentleman'. If he is played by an actor past middle age then it lends weight to the sense of his being separate from the young people whom he attempts to befriend. His separation is not simply a result of age, but of a preoccupation with the past; Rosalind and Orlando are pre-occupied with the present. Rosalind's wit is easily a match for that of her older companion. For all his travels Jaques has never really arrived anywhere, while Rosalind, also a traveller, believes she has found her destination in Orlando.

Although subsequently the scene is taken up with love games played out by Rosalind and Orlando, we should not forget when reading what they are given to say that throughout their discourse there is another silent but expressive character on stage with them: Celia. Her reactions to what is said and done by the lovers remind an audience in the theatre of the nature of this 'game', and of its implications. At times during the scene Rosalind becomes so carried away that she almost forgets that she is in the role of Ganymede. Twice she says: 'And I am your Rosalind', 'Am not I your Rosalind', as if daring and challenging Orlando to recognize her. She is perhaps frustrated that he does not and remains in ignorance perfectly willing to continue with the fiction.

Rosalind takes the game to its limits in the mock-marriage; here Celia is pressed into service as a reluctant priest. It is a very difficult role for her; indeed her whole situation is fraught with difficulty as she has to watch her very dearest friend's loyalty and love in the process of being transferred from her to a man, with the inevitable result that their childhood friendship will never be the same again. Rosalind's gain in this scene is Celia's loss. It is not simply because she knows it is wrong to mock by imitation a sacred ceremony that initially she says, 'I cannot say the words', in response to Rosalind's unthinking demand: 'Pray thee, marry us.' Apart from this one incident, where she is in fact *used* by Rosalind, her sense of being superfluous makes her angry. This feeling is fed by Rosalind's disparaging remarks about women, and by the end of the scene Rosalind's joy is counterbalanced for the audience by the display of Celia's hurt: 'You have simply misused our sex in your love-prate. We must have your doublet and hose plucked over your head, and show the world what the bird hath done to her own nest' (IV.1.186–9). Despite Rosalind's partial recognition of what has happened between the two women, and her attempts to win her friend back, the old intimacy of the two 'from their cradles bred together' is lost for ever. Adolescent needs have separated them. Thus, at the end of the scene, Rosalind goes to 'find a shadow and sigh till he come' and Celia, no longer having the same role to play in this relationship, says 'And I'll sleep.'

Act IV Scene 2

This short hunting scene has often given directors a headache. What to do with it is seen as a problem and a challenge. Recently Adrian Noble directed Fiona Shaw (as Celia) in a Jungian dream-fantasy, where she became the object of the hunt. Presumably the director's intention was to suggest the subconscious effect the pre-sexual wooing of Rosalind and Orlando was having on its witness – the impressionable Celia. Adrian Noble's production was for the Royal Shakespeare Company at Stratford-on-Avon in 1985. There, in the old theatre in the very first season, the 1879 production of *As You Like It* by Barry Sullivan required a stuffed stag to be carried across the stage in great solemnity as part of this scene. The beast had been killed in the nearby park at Charlecote. The appearance of the stuffed stag became a Stratford tradition for almost forty years until, in a production of the play in 1919, the director (the young Nigel Playfair) decided to rid the stage of the spectre of the, by now, moth-eaten beast. This, together with other changes to the traditional staging of the play, resulted in elaborate displays of disgust by Stratford audiences. When Playfair entered a public room in his hotel, fellow guests left it, and the cast as a whole were 'cut' in the streets of Stratford.[7]

John Dexter at the National Theatre in 1979 used the scene as an opportunity to display the 'festivals and rites of the countryside'. An animal sacrifice was deemed to have taken place and 'the innards of the slaughtered deer, formalized as a red garland, were entwined in the branches of the sacred tree, and the victorious William [who had killed the deer] was smeared on his chest and back with the deer's blood and crowned with its antlers, as other actors gathered round him wearing beautifully expressive deer masks.'[8]

Act IV Scene 3

The cousins are seen waiting for Orlando who is again late. Celia still seems troubled and to have little time for Rosalind's expressed anxieties: 'I warrant you, with pure love and troubled brain he hath ta'en his bow and arrows, and is gone forth to sleep' (IV.3.3–6). The waiting is interrupted by the arrival of Silvius bringing a letter from Phebe. He has been misled by her as to its contents, and is now in for a shock. Like Orlando, Phebe has been moved to write poetry to the one she loves. When Rosalind reads her verses aloud, the truth of what they mean is conveyed to Silvius. It is appropriate that his resulting sense of loss and disappointment is shared by Celia – 'Alas, poor shepherd!' But Rosalind has little sympathy for him and sends him off to confront Phebe, to 'charge her to love thee'.

Oliver's entrance brings on to the stage a character known to the audience but of course unknown to Rosalind and Celia. The encounter then becomes Celia's wooing scene. In their meeting it is suddenly Celia, not Rosalind, who is dominant, and it must be obvious in performance that Celia and Oliver have experienced 'love at first sight'. As Oliver tells his tale, for once Rosalind is the silent character. But as that tale unfolds, detailing how Orlando has risked his life for his brother and been wounded in the effort, her attention is suddenly sharply focused. Then, at the sight of the 'bloody napkin' (the intrusion of reality into what could otherwise be another fiction) Rosalind's ability to sustain her masculine role is overcome. Her feminine nature is now ascendent. It takes a good deal of prompting by Celia to remind Rosalind of the need to keep up the pretence. She calls on Ganymede twice, and then a third time, by which time she herself is so confused that although she still has the presence of mind to keep Rosalind's gender clear, she forgets their supposed relationship and calls: 'Cousin Ganymede', not brother! Rosalind's disguise almost slips away entirely, but she manages, with a great effort, and not at all convincingly, to sustain it. By contrasting the relative weakness of Rosalind with the strength and heroism of Orlando at this point, Shakespeare prepares the audience for the reassumption of the feminine part by Ganymede at the end of the play. Thus, after a period in which we have seen a woman act like a man, with 'masculine' qualities of wit and assertiveness, we now see a woman acting like an Elizabethan stereotype of how a woman ought to behave. Rosalind, on the brink of marriage, must now give up her authority and become passive. Accordingly she must be shown to be at the mercy of her feelings, confessing at the end of the scene: 'I should have been a woman by right.'

Act V Scene 1

Seeing Touchstone and Audrey immediately after hearing of the heroic action of Orlando, and having registered that another romance – between Celia and Oliver – is underway, brings the whole play once more back to earth with a bump. The world as experienced by the young lovers may be composed of lion-slaying heroes and princesses who faint in awe at their daring deeds; it may seem a magical place where, just as despair at the loss of a female friend sets in, a handsome and socially eligible man arrives to replace the lost companion; but it is also a world where, as Touchstone earlier remarks to Jaques, 'Man hath his desires.' So now, instead of an almost impossible fiction, we see the impatience of two very ordinary people when the fulfilment of their desire is frustrated.

It is a well-established formula in Shakespeare's comedy that lovers have to overcome obstacles to their happiness before they are permitted to achieve it. In this scene that convention is mocked. William is a potential obstacle to the happiness of Audrey and Touchstone. As Touchstone knows and says to Audrey, 'a youth here in the forest lays claim to you'. But Audrey, with her eye firmly fixed on the main chance, denies that William cares for her; 'he hath no interest in me in the world'. William flatly contradicts this:

TOUCHSTONE ... You do love this maid?
WILLIAM I do, sir.

(V.1.34–6)

Touchstone then proceeds to mock William as previously he mocked Corin. William, however, is not made of the same stuff as Silvius, and lamely gives up his claim by meekly departing – although he goes because Audrey and not Touchstone has asked him to.

Act V Scene 2

We now return to the magical world of the forest romance. The dialogue between the two brothers confirms their new-found amity, and the previous impression of the audience that Oliver and Celia are now also in love. In this romantic fairy-tale world, the audience has to accept that strange things happen. As Oliver remarks to his brother, 'Neither call the giddiness of it in question'. The 'sudden wooing' and 'sudden consenting' is also referred to by Rosalind, who, in stressing the mutual attraction of Celia and Oliver, acknowledges an underlying sexual drive: '. . . they made a pair of stairs to marriage which they will climb incontinent or else be incontinent before marriage' (V.2.36–8).

Reflecting, as they have been, on the behaviour of a cousin and a brother, the thoughts of Rosalind and Orlando now turn away from the games they have played and towards the prospect of the physical reality of their own love, and not just the mixed delights of the game of courtship. Orlando, having seen the prospect of his brother's satisfaction, cannot contain his own frustration and cries: 'I can live no longer by thinking.' Rosalind wisely decides to bring the charade to a conclusion, and proposes making a marriage quartet – a symbolic reuniting of both the cousins and the brothers. When Silvius and Phebe enter, the prospect of harmony is widened to include them, although it may well take the skill of one who professes she can 'do strange things' to bring it about. The chorus of all the as yet unsatisfied lovers should perhaps be sung, for, as Rosalind remarks, it sounds 'like the howling of Irish wolves against the moon'. But despite the apparent discord, Rosalind will effect harmony. She is in no doubt as to the eventual outcome and reminds her company: 'I have left you commands.'

Act V Scene 3

Not only are the high and mighty preparing for marriage, but, quite independently of any magic of Rosalind, Touchstone and Audrey know that, for them too, 'Tomorrow is the joyful day.' The delightful song sung by the two pages is none the less a piece of pastoral poetry held up to ridicule. The romantic lyric 'It was a lover and his lass' is sung to Touchstone and Audrey, the most *unromantic* of couples. To Touchstone the song is pointless ('there was no great matter in the ditty') and a waste of time ('I count it but time lost to hear such a foolish song'). To the audience, however, the song is delightful, an atmospheric preparation for the mood of the final scene.

Act V Scene 4

Although the scene begins and ends in the forest, by the end of the action the thoughts of all the visitors to Arden have turned, once again, towards the court – their real home and their *natural* environment. The holiday world is at an end; it is time to return to the world of work.

> If all the year were playing holidays,
> To sport would be as tedious as to work;
> *Henry IV Part 1* (I.2.202–3)

To an audience consisting of her father, future husband and members of the court-in-exile, Rosalind performs her last independent action of the play. Her final words as Ganymede prefigure those uttered by Jaques before his departure for the dark cave, and before the final departure of the actors from the stage. After Rosalind has left, taking Celia with her, there is a short comic interlude in which Touchstone is the leading light. What he says is amusing but, like so much else of what he says, it also reveals the emptiness and fallibility of language. The play needs this break in the action. It helps to turn the minds of the audience back to the court (and Touchstone's references are to courtly behaviour), and also, on a practical level, it gives the actors playing Ganymede and Aliena the necessary time to transform themselves back into the figures of Rosalind and Celia, both now dressed for marriage.

At the moment when Hymen enters – a role necessitated by Rosalind's return to womanhood, which precludes her from having the authority she previously possessed as Ganymede – the whole mood of the scene changes. There is a sense of mystery and magic about this character, no doubt heightened in performance by his appearance (probably originally clad in the traditional saffron-coloured robe associated with the god).

The stage directions have him represented by 'a masquer'. This entry into what is still a pastoral setting signals unequivocally to the audience (on stage *and* in the theatre) that a change of location is imminent; they should be prepared to leave the world of the country and return to their own world of the town. Masques were entertainments designed for a very different world from that of the Forest of Arden. They were lavish and highly contrived entertainments characterized by formal and elaborate costumes, and full of visual spectacle. All this was created without regard to cost, as an important part of their function was to impress upon the visitor the material wealth and taste of the patron of the masque – the monarch. At the same time they acted as a reassurance to the court itself.

Nothing could be further from the representation of pastoral simplicity expounded by Duke Senior at the beginning of Act II. The appearance of Hymen heralds a world not of 'shady bowers' but of 'painted pomp'. It is, of course, the 'natural' environment for a Duke. Now, at last, the evidence of eyes can be relied upon as disguise is cast off and Rosalind moves first to her startled father and then to her future husband. Hymen now 'must make conclusion/Of these most strange events' (V.4.23–4) and, to cover the time in which the pairs of lovers tell their stories to one another (the audience already know the details) a song – that traditional symbol of harmony and *social* regeneration – is sung.

But, as the sudden and unexpected entrance of Jaques de Boys reminds us, despite the union of eight hands in marriage, harmony is not yet complete. Only with the arrival of Jaques de Boys, the second son of old Sir Rowland, and brother to Orlando and Oliver, is an end in sight. Outrageously contrived though his entry may seem to contemporary audiences, used to conventions of naturalistic presentation, we should remember that the mood of the scene, and of the play as a whole, is one of a fairy-story, not a documentary. What Jaques de Boys does is to give the news that makes the actual return to the court possible. Duke Frederick, hunting his brother on the fringes of Arden, has, in this charmed place, met with 'an old religious man' who has succeeded in reforming him. As a result he decides to give up the material world altogether. He leaves behind 'painted pomp' and takes up the solitary contemplative life. But his conversion gives back to Duke Senior what was once his by right: his crown and lands.

The new ruler, or rather the old ruler now restored to his rightful and natural position of temporal authority, addresses his subjects. Before finally leaving the holiday world and taking on the cares and responsibilities of office, there will be one last chance to celebrate in the carefree way of the forest. In the spirit of this place their revelry will be 'rustic', not courtly.

Only Jaques stands out from the harmonious picture, and it is fitting that he should. He, after all, will not return to the court; his life is not to be transformed, he is too old and perhaps too cynical to change. The joy and hope of the lovers is something he cannot share, any more than he is willing to partake of the responsibilities thrust back upon Duke Senior. Despite the Duke's pleas for him to remain and return with them all to the court, he decides to stay in the forest and keep company with the newly self-exiled Duke Frederick.

Finally, the actor playing Rosalind addresses the audience. He (or she) breaks the illusion and encourages the listeners to applaud. It is time for everyone – actors, audiences and readers – to leave the holiday world of the play and go home.

2. A Romantic Text

The first of my imaginary directors is a man. He is well-established in the theatre and takes his general, philosophical approach to the study of the text from what he learnt as a Cambridge undergraduate under F. R. Leavis in the late 1950s. He is very happy with the traditional view that sees *As You Like It* as a pastoral romance. His *As You Like It* reverberates with the echoes of an Oxford don, Dame Helen Gardner, who in a lecture to undergraduates on a sunny summer morning spoke of the play as a comedy:

The great symbol of pure comedy is marriage, by which the world is renewed, and its endings are always instinct with a sense of fresh beginnings. Its rhythm is the rhythm of the life of mankind, which goes on and renews itself as the life of nature does. The rhythm of tragedy, on the other hand, is the rhythm of the individual life which comes to a close, and its great symbol is death.[9]

He firmly believes that this play is *relevant* to the latter half of the twentieth century; relevant because it reminds its audience of lasting, permanent values which must not be allowed to be overcome by what the director feels fervently, if not originally, are the 'barbarians at the gate'. His production will attempt to show that *As You Like It* contains a message of hope, optimism and faith in 'the power of the human spirit' to overcome obstacles and continually regenerate itself.

The company, consisting of actors and technicians and stage management, who have been brought together to create this performance-text of *As You Like It*, first meet in a warm, purpose-built rehearsal room somewhere in the bowels of one of our prestigious national theatres. Most of the company have worked together before and frequently under the same director, who is now preparing to speak to them. What he has to say appears to be entirely spontaneous and 'off the cuff'. In fact, his speech is a carefully contrived peroration – the result of many concentrated hours in the study prior to this official start to the collective rehearsal process.

In this 'key-note' speech to the cast, our first director hopes both to inspire and provide his team with a coherent intellectual framework within which individual performances can develop harmoniously. He sees the role of the director first and foremost as carrying overall responsibility for laying down guidelines for all subsequent action. While in one sense wishing to encourage the 'creativity' of the actors, hoping that they will invent and contribute ideas of their own, ultimately this 'romantic' director will only adopt those ideas if they do not conflict with the masterplan for the finished performance-text he is about to describe. He begins with a personal (and pastoral) memory.

It may at first seem rather odd, even perverse, but I hope you will all bear with me if I begin today, our first rehearsal of this great play, by talking briefly not about it, or about Shakespeare, but about myself! As some of you already know, I was born in a large Edwardian house in East Anglia. We were not a wealthy household; the house itself had been bought a few months after the end of the Second World War at a knock-down price by my family, who, having invested their life-savings (and my father's war invalidity pension) into it, intended to run it as a boarding house, or 'private hotel', as my mother preferred to think of it. My family not unnaturally predicted that after the stress and strain of a long war people would need holidays. And they did – at least at first.

In the short summer 'season', from mid-July to mid-September, we were fully booked with people; mostly families from the Midlands whose new prosperity stemmed from the rapidly developing car and motor-component factories, in which mass-produced products they usually arrived. 'Guests' stayed for a week (a fortnight's holiday was still a long way off in those days) and had 'full board' for £7; children half-price. We were, I still recall, proud of what we gave them for their money – huge fried breakfasts, fresh crab teas, black pudding, roast meat and, as our advertisement in the town guidebook proudly proclaimed, 'Hot and cold in every room'.

Alas, the boom was short-lived. The end of the 1950s saw the introduction of cheap air travel and longer holidays. The promise of unlimited sunshine began to lure our previously loyal clients into the clutches of the burgeoning 'package holiday' trade. The charms of a day spent day-dreaming in a deckchair on the pier, ignoring the bite of the wind off the North Sea, were cast off in favour of views of the Mediterranean glimpsed from a balcony high up in a new multi-storied, purpose-built hotel. Eventually we had to give up, close down and move out.

Looking back, the house itself was a great place to spend childhood. Now, more than thirty years on, it seems to me, to borrow a phrase from *As You Like It*, a 'golden world'. The house still comes regularly and unbidden into my imagination and my dreams. It appears as a place full of long corridors and endless large rooms, all with seemingly limitless potential for exploration during the two thirds and more of the year in which they remained empty. When occupied they were full of new and exciting faces – holiday faces – people who for a short span were free of day-to-day responsibilities and the cares that went with them. Their holiday happiness was freely extended to include me on 'outings'; we shared sandwiches in beach huts half-full with fine sand. Their brief respite from the world of work, and the house itself, provided a continual holiday world for me: one which on some levels it seems I have always been trying to regain. Looking back it seems that like Rosalind in Arden I was always in a 'holiday humour'.

But, as you know, childhood memories are notoriously unreliable and highly selective; mine are no exception. A few years ago I happened to be in the town itself and noticed that the old house was up for sale. I decided then and there to assume the role of prospective buyer in order to have the chance of looking over it once more. Needless to say, the experience was a terrible disappointment. Everything now seemed small, even cramped; the acres of my memory were immediately reduced to very domestic proportions. The rooms (there were only six bedrooms) were close together, and the staircases and corridors narrow and short. I very rapidly gave up looking and retreated, hoping sincerely that not too much damage had been inflicted on my comfortable and obviously, at some level, *necessary* image of my seaside arcadia. My memory of what was there was infinitely preferable to the reality. I had created a personal myth – a pastoral world – out of some obscure but powerful need and did not intend to compromise its integrity by undertaking field-work into its origins, or readily to relinquish it.

I suspect most of you have a memory of childhood where, like me – to complete the quotation from our play – you did 'fleet the time carelessly as they did in the golden world'. If you have no such comfortable memory to tap when you feel the need to escape from the pressures of the present, you may well substitute a dream of the future for one of the past. An ideal future, like my idealized past, can banish care; there things which now seem fraught with difficulty become either unimportant or effortless. In such idealized times and places people are genuine in their regard for one another, not false and dissembling. Common to us all is the need to escape from reality from time to time. We need, and therefore must invent, a different kind of world from that which we currently inhabit. Let us, along with Shakespeare, call it the Forest of Arden.

So this first director sees in *As You Like It* what he chooses to call a 'holiday world', in which the young in particular experience a joyous freedom that is infectious. In doing so he is following, consciously or unconsciously, a well-established critical and theatrical tradition, which sees the play as a Romantic comedy. Perhaps he has had his attention drawn to that most influential book on the comedies by C. L. Barber, *Shakespeare's Festive Comedy*, in which the author speaks of the forest:

The Forest of Arden, like the wood outside Athens, is a region defined by an attitude of liberty from ordinary limitations, a festive place where the folly of romance can have its day.[10]

Let us now try to explore and elaborate a reading of *As You Like It* that supports this directorial approach and sees in the text an optimistic message of the power of love to regenerate a fallen world.

The Forest of Arden of the Romantic tradition is indeed a kind of holiday world, complete with its visitors and residents. Of course, like any kind of resort, it appears very different to its two main groups of inhabitants – the natives and the tourists. Arden has its own residents, who presumably continued to live and die there long after Duke Senior, his merry men, Rosalind, Orlando, Celia, Oliver, Touchstone and the rest returned to their life at court. For make no mistake, the courtiers' natural environment is at court, not in the forest. During their temporary stay Arden becomes a very special kind of place in which these sojourners enjoy a freedom missing in the world they have recently left behind. It is a freedom the audience can appreciate all the more because they have witnessed the lack of it in the opening action set in the court of Duke Frederick. What we see in the forest is *freedom from* the constraints of a 'tyrant Duke'.

In preparing for this production the director gives a great deal

of time and thought to the problems of casting. Building o
idea that Arden is a place of freedom from the responsib
associated with living in a society, and that the lovers, Rosalind
and Orlando, experience this freedom keenly, he wants to cast
actors who can project an air of youthful innocence and enthusiasm. He sees their youth and, in particular, the critical time in
both their lives at which Shakespeare chooses to introduce them
as very significant pointers in helping the audience to understand
his reading of the text. Rosalind and Orlando have to be played
as adolescents, for both are at an in-between stage; no longer
children, yet not fully adult. Initially, therefore, both are to be
seen as socially marginal. Rosalind is financially kept by the
Duke, and Orlando by his brother. For Rosalind, being fully
adult is synonymous with being a married woman; for Orlando
it is having the means (which his brother denies him) to control
and fully determine his life in society. Before they enter Arden
both are on the brink of leaving childhood behind. When they
leave the forest the transition to maturity has been accomplished
and they return to the world as fully fledged adults. The
director's view is confirmed when he notes that prior to making
this transition the young adolescent Rosalind chooses quite
coolly to stay away from her natural father until she has been
able to explore her new-found freedom and use it to get what
she wants. When she finally does reveal herself to her father it is
to present him with a *fait accompli* – she is no longer just his
daughter but a woman about to become independent of him for
ever.

In this in-between time, the director argues, there is often a
feeling of tremendous relief, which comes from being free of
past constraints. He urges Rosalind and Orlando to think about
the prospect of life in Arden as they would about leaving home
for the very first time to live independently. He wants them to
see the forest as what he calls an 'enabling place'. While there,
neither has to acknowledge any parental authority that might
seek to govern their behaviour. When once again in contact with
her natural father, Rosalind's sense of new-found freedom
overcomes her desire and curiosity to resume her role as
daughter:

41

ROSALIND I met the Duke yesterday and had much question with him. He asked me of what parentage I was. I told him, of as good as he – so he laughed and let me go.

(III.4.31–4)

In the Forest of Arden the young people are really free for the first time in their lives, and free in a way people of their class never could be in the society of the court. Rosalind and Celia are in a sense doubly free; free from authority figures (fathers) and also, by means of disguises, free from their social roles as young women of the court. Now, in the forest and at this stage in their lives they also seem to have endless time ('there's no clock in the forest').

In the rehearsals the actors playing Rosalind, Celia, Orlando and Oliver are all encouraged, through a series of improvisations designed by the director, to *play*. They play half-forgotten games of childhood – blind man's buff, tag, and even postman's knock. They also come to rehearsal one morning to find that the stage-management has provided a large trunk full of an assortment of hats, dresses, cloaks, shoes and jackets, with which they are urged to play at 'dressing up'. Our director believes that, once in Arden, what Rosalind in particular indulges in is game-playing. She plays hard, like the child she has so recently been. One of the scenes improvised is that between Rosalind and Celia in Act I when, following the Duke's threat to the friendship of the young women, they devise a means of escape, which takes them straight back to childhood. They pretend to be someone else, and effect that transformation by dressing up. Their plan itself is almost a cliché of childhood: they decide to run away from home. This is the exchange on which the director focuses:

CELIA

    I'll put myself in poor and mean attire
    And with a kind of umber smirch my face.
    The like do you; so shall we pass along
    And never stir assailants.
ROSALIND   Were it not better,
    Because that I am more than common tall,
    That I did suit me all points like a man?

A gallant curtle-axe upon my thigh,
A boar-spear in my hand, and in my heart
Lie there what hidden woman's fear there will,
We'll have a swashing and a martial outside,
As many other mannish cowards have
That do outface it with their semblances.

CELIA

What shall I call thee when thou art a man?

ROSALIND

I'll have no worse a name than Jove's own page,
And therefore look you call me 'Ganymede'.
But what will you be called?

CELIA

Something that hath a reference to my state:
No longer 'Celia', but 'Aliena'.

(I.3.109–26)

The actors soon catch the enthusiasm and energy in this exchange that drives the two young women into exile and to a
grand adventure. It generates tremendous excitement by means
of the enormously fast transition from despair to hope and even
optimism in what the future holds. The action moves from
Celia's hopeless cry: 'O my poor Rosalind, wither wilt thou go?',
to her strong, confident boast at the close of the scene: 'Now go
we in content/To liberty, and not to banishment' (I.3.135–6). In
their work on the scene, both actresses are encouraged to be
very intimate and tactile. Like young girls who are genuinely
close friends they constantly touch and hold hands. This kind of
gestural language is intended by the director to be in sharp
contrast to the earlier public scenes at the court where convention required a very different and more formal code of behaviour
between the two.

When Rosalind, Celia and Touchstone eventually arrive in
Arden they are, by contrast, tired and somewhat dispirited with
the exuberance of planning. Neither of the women is keen to put
off her disguise; by continuing the pretence they sustain the child-
ish connection. As children learn, they are learning about themselves, other people and the world at large – through imitation
or mimesis. Indeed the actress playing Rosalind spends some of
her time preparing for her role by carefully considering just how
much Rosalind learns and therefore changes during her time in

Arden. The director certainly wants the audience to see a near-child at the beginning of the performance and a woman at its close. Rosalind learns a lot about the human condition in the forest. She learns in particular about the nature of the phenomenon called love; not only what it is like to love and to be loved in return, but also, by watching Silvius and Phebe, she sees something of what it is like to suffer unrequited love – to experience love as something cruel and potentially destructive. Rosalind's disguise allows her the luxury of observing the world at a distance. She can and does try out her own feelings whilst remaining secure and secret behind the mask of Ganymede.

Celia too is someone who learns by observation facilitated by disguise. She is an almost constant observer of the love-play between Rosalind and Orlando, and though at the time she appears to find it disturbing:

You have simply misused our sex in your love-prate. We must have your doublet and hose plucked over your head, and show the world what the bird hath done to her own nest.

(IV.1.186–9)

she nevertheless continually observes and learns from what she sees. Celia's ability to recognize true love when it happens to *her* late in the action, and in the superficially unlikely form of Oliver – many critics in the past have thought him unworthy of her – is thanks to the education in love granted her by being able to observe Rosalind and Orlando.

In rehearsals it becomes clear that Celia plays a vital role in the courtship scenes between Rosalind and Orlando. Although she has few lines to speak at this time, Celia generates a powerful textual response by guiding the audience in the theatre towards the director's desired effect through her reactions and responses to what the pair of lovers say and do. For example, when rehearsing IV.1 Rosalind becomes more and more daring in her role-playing as Ganymede. She pushes, tugs and physically holds Orlando and even, at one point, almost kisses him. Celia's concern – visible to the audience but not to the lovers – serves to remind them of the risk Rosalind is running – of the distance she has travelled from the normal behaviour of a young woman of breeding. For the actors, too, Celia proves to be important. Her presence gives both of them, and especially Rosalind, someone to play to; an audience able to observe and judge – because she knows the true identity of the role-player – the skill and daring of the performance.

The director encourages the players to see the forest as a schoolroom which a usually strict teacher has left temporarily unsupervised. Through the resulting play they learn a great deal more about life than when they were being taught formally.

The idea of the schoolroom is useful, for Rosalind herself acts as a teacher to the unschooled Orlando, who has been kept 'rustically at home' by a brother who 'mines my gentility with my education' (I.1.18–19). It is Rosalind who deliberately prolongs their courtship and sustains her disguise, both to school Orlando and also to test his sincerity and suitability as a future husband. Rosalind has fallen in love with this young man not because he has displayed any of the usual attributes of the gentlemen she has seen in her uncle's court, but because she has seen in him his *inner* quality – what he identifies as 'the spirit of my father, which I think is within me' (I.1.20). But this noble nature needs to be nurtured and during the process Orlando must be taught by Rosalind, in her disguise as Ganymede, *how* to woo. He imitates what little he has seen of courtly behaviour and hopes it will be appropriate, but although in some respects he adopts the right *form* of behaviour – he apes the traditional Elizabethan device of writing poetry to his love – the execution of it leads to very poor verse indeed. Bad verse would, perhaps, be of little consequence if the results of such labours remained on the trees and never reached the beloved herself. But the gesture is paramount, for it is all part of Orlando acting out his inner state of being in love. And because he is unschooled in the ways of the court (the world of 'painted pomp'), he is a bad actor and does not display, as Rosalind laughingly points out to him, the elaborate guise that shouts to all the world when a courtier is supposedly in love:

ORLANDO What were his marks?
ROSALIND A lean cheek, which you have not; a blue eye and sunken, which you have not; an unquestionable spirit, which you have not; a beard neglected,

45

which you have not – but I pardon you for that, for simply your having in beard is a younger brother's revenue. Then your hose should be ungartered, your bonnet unbanded, your sleeve unbuttoned, your shoe untied, and everything about you demonstrating a careless desolation. But you are no such man.[11]

(III.2.357–66)

What Rosalind is describing here is highly contrived behaviour designed for the display of love, and far removed from the spontaneous reactions she so much admires and values in the behaviour of Orlando. She is secretly delighted that he *is* 'no such man'; he has no need to act what he genuinely feels. In this way the play raises questions about the nature of sophisticated behaviour. Shakespeare often does this. Hamlet, for instance, also finds the conventional modes of expression inadequate:

> I have that within which passes show –
> These but the trappings and suits of woe.
> (*Hamlet* I.2.85–6)

Paradoxically, it is Rosalind's acting – being false in pretending to be Ganymede – that gives Orlando the chance to be natural and to display to his love what he truly feels in his heart. If not exactly a voyeur, Rosalind certainly has the advantage over Orlando; after all, he never gets to see her in an unguarded or unprepared moment as she does him. Much of what he learns depends on her support, knowledge and her resulting power to control. Orlando is given the opportunity – rare for a man – to take an essentially passive role in courtship. The traditional roles here are fundamentally reversed.

But if Orlando is to be socially acceptable as a mate for Rosalind, he must learn more than how to be a lover, and Rosalind is not his only teacher. From Adam, too, he learns a lot. Our director tells the cast of one production in which Adam was shown in scene 1 teaching Orlando to wrestle! Certainly by his own example he teaches him about the values of the past, and that the values of the 'antique world' are superior to those of the present-day world of Duke Frederick's court.

ORLANDO

O good old man, how well in thee appears
The constant service of the antique world,

When service sweat for duty, not for meed!
(II.3.56–8)

Adam connects Orlando with his past (he was servant to his father) and in doing so opens up the future. It is because Adam has shown one of the cardinal virtues (thrift) that there is money to enable Orlando even to contemplate an alternative life. The old man demonstrates that, despite appearances to the contrary, ideals and values have not been entirely destroyed, although both teacher and pupil will need to leave the harsh and degenerate climate of Oliver's household in order to re-establish or re-discover them elsewhere. Orlando learns that he must model himself not on his brother, but on his late father and his friend, the exiled Duke Senior. Indeed it is from the banished Duke that Orlando learns one very important lesson about the nature of life in society, albeit a society in the forest not in a court.

In Act II scene 7, Orlando leaves the weakened Adam to search for food and comes across a gathering of men in the forest. Of course Orlando knows nothing about them; he cannot know that they are the followers of his father's old friend, nor whether they will be friendly or hostile towards him. All he sees is his own need to secure food for Adam. Based on his past experience of the world, Orlando presumes that those with material possessions (in this case the food that is conspicuously displayed before him) will not readily share them. Assuming his need will be met with hostility, Orlando barges into their presence, dispensing with civilities and demanding all those before him to 'Forbear, and eat no more.' He goes so far as to threaten death to anyone who touches the food. The tension of this encounter is diffused in rehearsals by the director's idea of having the actor playing Jaques ignore the apparent threat and instead respond: 'An you will not be answered with reason [pronounced raisin], I must die,' while taking a grape from a large bunch and eating it.[12] The Duke seizes the moment:

DUKE

What would you have? Your gentleness shall force,
More than your force move us to gentleness.

ORLANDO

I almost die for food, and let me have it.

DUKE
  Sit down and feed, and welcome to our table.
ORLANDO
  Speak you so gently? Pardon me, I pray you.
  I thought that all things had been savage here
                    (II.7.104–108, my italics)

From this practical demonstration of compassion Orlando learns that it *is* possible for men to act in their collective interests in a civilized and unselfish way. It is perhaps because of this incident that he too, later in the action, is able to act with great compassion, first forgiving and then saving the life of his brother. For when Oliver gives his account to the astonished Rosalind and Celia of the slaying of the lioness by Orlando, the audience in the theatre as well as those on stage are able to acknowledge something very significant about the young man:

ROSALIND
  But to Orlando: did he leave him there,
  Food to the sucked and hungry lioness?
OLIVER
  Twice did he turn his back and purposed so.
  But *kindness, nobler ever than revenge,*
  And nature, stronger than his just occasion,
  Made him give battle to the lioness,
  Who quickly fell before him . . .
                    (IV.3.126–32, my italics)

For the director of this Romantic production, the recounting of this act of courage and magnanimity is confirmation that Orlando has passed his final exam. He is now a man, not a boy, and a man fit to inherit his father's status. He has learnt about love, about compassion, about the values of duty and service, and finally about forgiveness and reconciliation. Thus Orlando has fulfilled the requirements of Romantic comedy, demonstrating both through words and actions that he is fit and ready for Rosalind. His nature has been nurtured in the hospitable pastoral environment of the Forest of Arden. The happy ending, complete with wedding, can now take place in the expectation that their marriage will produce children who will faithfully continue to uphold the values of their parents.

  As you will have noted, this performance-text has been very

much centred on the role of the lovers, and on the power of their love to redirect a world floundering in jaded middle age towards hope in a rejuvenated future. In this production characters like Phebe and Silvius, Audrey and Touchstone exist very much as supporting players to the central character Rosalind. She is the undoubted 'star' of this and probably any Romantic production, and indeed on her hangs the eventual happy and affirmative resolution of the action.

It is a portrait of a young woman in love that our director is seeking to create and leave fresh in the minds of the audience. He wants them to remember 'his' Rosalind in the way in which he himself recalls seeing Vanessa Redgrave play the part in Michael Elliott's RSC production of the play in 1961. In his mind's eye he can still recall, along with the critics, a Rosalind who:

... snatches off her cap so that her hair tumbles like a flock of goldfinches into sunshine ...

(J. W. Lambert, *The Sunday Times* 9 July 1961)

and

... is a creature of fire and light, her voice a golden gate opening on lapiz-lazuli hinges, her body a slender supple reed rippling in the breeze of her love ...

(Bernard Levin, *The Daily Express* 5 July 1961)

At first sight (the designer had been told to prepare a location which was cool in tone, suggesting the 'barren desert' rather than the 'green corn field' and the 'acres of the rye') the Forest of Arden seems an unlikely setting for a holiday romance. Rosalind arrives there in the depths of a bitter winter when, as Duke Senior remarks, the cruel wind '... bites and blows upon my body/Even till I shrink with cold' (II.1.8–9). Yet by the time that the Duke is ready to leave his place of exile the climate has changed. The lighting designer gradually softens the harsh lights of the early scenes in the forest and allows a build up of colour and warmth to flood the stage. Spring, and the promise of a fruitful summer, has come at last. It is the driving energy of Rosalind's love for Orlando which the director seeks to show as responsible for the transformation of this hostile environment, turning it instead into something welcoming and hospitable. So too it is the power of the love within him that gives Orlando strength to overcome the natural dangers of this place in the shape of the lioness. Just as the cycle of the natural world keeps on turning and 'every winter turns to spring', so life in the forest is regenerated through the *warmth* of true feelings expressed there. These feelings are what unify, reconcile and provide the exiles with the strength and vision to return and reform the social world from which they fled. The culminating symbol of this transformation, the pre-marriage, is staged with much use of music. (There are in fact more songs in *As You Like It* than in any other play by Shakespeare, and a popular 'folk-rock' band composes and performs them for the production.) In showing a detailed preparation for marriage the director wants to stress that the celebration is a rite of passage, symbolizing harmony, completeness and faith in the regeneration of the human species.

The Forest of Arden can sometimes seem a labyrinth, and in emphasizing Rosalind's triumph over circumstances our director does not entirely forget what he calls 'the darker side' of the play. As a young man in the 1960s he had read, along with many of his contemporaries in the theatre, Jan Kott's book *Shakespeare Our Contemporary*.[13] Although he now disagrees with most of it he none the less recalls the chapter on the comedies, 'Shakespeare's Bitter Arcadia', in which Kott speaks about *Twelfth Night* and *As You Like It* as being generally

considered the most romantic of the Comedies. But of all the 'contemporary reactions' to Shakespeare, from Elizabethan times to ours, the romantic was the most false and the one that left behind it the most fatal theatrical tradition.[14]

Indeed, love in *As You Like It* does not triumph without a struggle. Rosalind and Orlando are *hunted* into the forest by Duke Frederick and Oliver and if they are caught, presumably death would follow:

DUKE FREDERICK [to Rosalind]
You, cousin,
Within these ten days if that thou beest found
So near our public court as twenty miles,
Thou diest for it.

(I.3.40.43)

DUKE FREDERICK [to Oliver]
 . . . look to it,
 Find out thy brother wheresoe'er he is,
 Seek him with candle, bring him dead or living
 Within this twelvemonth, or turn no more
 To seek a living in our territory.

(III.1.4–8)

Not all the threats to the happiness of the young people are external. Our director connects the character of Jaques with that of Shakespeare's other brooding observer of the world's follies: Prince Hamlet. Like Hamlet, the Jaques of this production dresses entirely in black. This is indicative of his inner state of melancholy and also seems to draw the audience's attention on to him whenever he appears on stage with others. The actor playing Jaques constantly tries to remind the audience that not everyone in Arcadia is susceptible to youth's power to charm and delight. He is presented as a thorn that threatens to puncture the idea of Arden as a kind of other-Eden – a pastoral paradise in which, because time does not exist, no one grows old and one can for ever breathe

> . . . the hospitable air of Arden, where convenient caves stand ready to receive outlaws, alfresco meals are abundantly provided, with a concert of birds and running brooks, and there is no worse hardship than a salubrious winter wind. This is 'the golden world' to which, with the beginning of his second act, Shakespeare at once transports us, such a world as has been the dream of poets since at least the time of Virgil when, wearied with the fooling and wranglings of society, they yearn for the simplicity and innocence of what they choose to think is man's natural state.[15]

The actor playing Jaques achieves a mood of world-weary cynicism, which, perhaps because it corresponds to his experience of the world of the court, pleases the exiled Duke but is firmly repudiated by Orlando and Rosalind. The lovers are full of hope and expectations; Jaques is empty of both. When Orlando and Jaques meet in the forest they do not share common ground. In this production the director has them enter with Orlando slightly in front, walking briskly, with Jaques struggling to keep up. It is obvious that Orlando has no desire for this particular company, and eventually Jaques is prompted to give up and leave Orlando to himself:

JAQUES I thank you for your company, but, good faith, I had as lief have been myself alone.
ORLANDO And so had I; but yet, for fashion sake, I thank you too for your society.
JAQUES God buy you, let's meet as little as we can.
ORLANDO I do desire we may be better strangers.

(III.2.246–51)

It is not long before Jaques is again on the receiving end of a rebuff. At the beginning of Act IV Rosalind has no time for this 'melancholy fellow'. Indeed the lovers and the melancholic are at opposite poles; the former *share* love of one another, the latter loves himself. Jaques is distanced from other people by his apparent conviction that all human social behaviour is ultimately based on pretence: the world is a stage, people players. By implication Jaques sees himself as alone amongst men in being no actor. Because he believes he can see the 'truth' of other people's duplicity, he is isolated from them; he is an outsider. Of course this is arrogant and nihilistic (Jaques also carefully contrives the role of the melancholy man). His cool and pessimistic approach to life is entirely unsuited to the company of a young man or woman in love. He is world-weary; those who are about to embark on a voyage of discovery in the world, as are Rosalind and Orlando, do not relish being told at the start that their journey will end up on the rocks:

JAQUES Yes, I have gained my experience.
ROSALIND And your experience makes you sad. I had rather have a fool to make me merry than experience to make me sad . . .

(IV.1.24–6)

Jaques mistrusts love. Perhaps he does not believe it exists at all, but rather is yet another role adopted by people at particular stages in their lives. Perhaps he is unable to recognize and accept love because, unlike his pessimism, love occurs spontaneously. In *As You Like It*, and indeed in other comedies by Shakespeare, love is characterized by the suddenness of overpowering feelings. It is, as young Lysander says in *A Midsummer Night's Dream*:

> Brief as the lightning in the collied night,
> That in a spleen unfolds both heaven and earth,
> And – ere a man hath power to say 'Behold!' –
> The jaws of darkness do devour it up.
>
> (I.1.145–8)

In the state of being in love shown in this production of *As You Like It*, reason and caution (associated with experience of the world) are secondary to feelings and emotions (associated with being young). Of course there is always danger when the 'heart rules the head', for, as Lysander knows despite his youth, 'So quick bright things come to confusion'.

This sense of love as a state of confusion into which the individual falls, rather than stepping carefully, is encapsulated in what happens to the lovers at the time of the wrestling match. In rehearsals this is given a good deal of time and attention. Charles is played by an ex-professional wrestler and Orlando spends a lot of time in running and weight-training in order to prepare for a realistic bout with him. The director uses as many actors in the scene as he can, for he wants to stress that it is the first *public* occasion in the action, and therefore an opportunity to show the court of Duke Frederick and the kind of entertainment it was accustomed to seeing. Earlier in this performance the audience has seen Orlando and Oliver wrestling with words, and indeed seen Orlando throw his brother to the ground on the line: 'I am no villain' (I.1.53). Now they see Charles overthrown and, in another sense, Rosalind too.

ROSALIND
> Sir, you have wrestled well, and overthrown
> More than your enemies.
>
> (I.2.243–4)

The actress inserts a long pause after 'overthrown', as if Rosalind almost regrets what she has already said and tries to stop herself from completing it. It is indeed a bold declaration for a young woman to make to a young man of apparently low social status. But Rosalind has *fallen* in love and, when that happens, there follows a temporary surrender of rationality and control. For Rosalind, love is letting go, a giving-up of the self to another.

Preserving control of himself is crucial to Jaques's well-being. The director spends a lot of time discussing the role with the actor who plays him. In particular they consider the famous speech beginning 'All the world's a stage'. The actor is worried by it because he feels that all the audience will immediately know what he is going to say before he says it, and that they will also anticipate the speech in the action. How can it possibly sound 'fresh' when it is probably amongst the best-known lines Shakespeare ever wrote? 'Everything seems to stop', the actor remarks, 'as soon as Jaques gets going. It's like performing a well-known aria in an opera and stopping for the applause.'[16]

In fact it is from the actor's fear of the speech as a 'set-piece' that he and the director decide to approach it. It is, they surmised, Jaques's cynicism that isolates him and prevents him from loving anyone. Unlike Rosalind and Orlando, he is incapable of 'letting go' and therefore his response to the world is closed to the spontaneous reactions that characterize love. Director and actor alike see the great speech as not only disproved by the actions of the play but also as demonstrating a rehearsed and carefully contrived world-view. It is anything but a spontaneous reaction and indeed sounds, in performance, as if it has been carefully composed in the solitary glades of the forest, well away from the society of people.

Although what Jaques says is superficially true – life *is* a progression from birth to death – what the director considers important is not the ability to describe the journey, however eloquently, but whether or not to attribute any *significance* to it. The director does not want the audience to be able to sit back and wallow in the poetry; he wants them to listen to what is said and to see it as the jaundiced view of a man who has distanced himself from the world because he lacks the essential spirit that feeds the play's overall optimism about the human condition. It is the *spirit* embodied in young lovers that informs life's passage and lifts it out of the routine, inevitable, 'strange eventful history' described by Jaques.

In this production it is clear that there is an alliance of the old and the young. Adam, Rosalind and Orlando have a spirit that invests their lives with significance. Adam does what he does not for his own self-interest or for reward but in accordance with the values of the 'antique world'. Hence a set of abstract ideals is made concrete and real through his altruism. Adam is capable of love – he loves Orlando; he loved old Sir Rowland. Unlike Jaques, he is not locked into a prison of self-love. The old man is proof that people can be other than self-interested and self-regarding, despite Jaques's assertions to the contrary. Significance *can* be invested in human behaviour by the manner in which it is conducted. At the end of a great and famous set speech, which effectively says that life has no meaning, the audience is confronted with a real as opposed to a rhetorical image, which contradicts what Jaques has been saying. If Adam is in his second childhood, then it is a very positive state to be in and far from 'mere oblivion'. What's more, he shares it with Rosalind and Orlando. In our Romantic *As You Like It* the young and the old have most in common and stare across a great divide on the other side of which are the representatives of middle age: Jaques and Duke Senior.

The actors playing Jaques and Duke Senior in this production both feel that they have a good deal in common, and that the Duke's almost equally well-known speech at the beginning of Act II, when the audience see Arden for the first time, has more than a passing resemblance to a good deal of what Jaques later says. You will remember that the Duke speaks with a kind of pride at being an 'outsider', subject to hardship and free from the world of 'painted pomp' that is the court of his brother. Above all it seems to be the artificiality and superficial behaviour of courtiers, or people in 'society', which concerns him most. It appals Duke Senior, just as Jaques is appalled by human social intercourse, which he describes using the apt metaphor of the artifice employed by an actor. In the Duke's great speech (Act II.2.1–17) he is thankful that in the forest, unlike the court, they feel 'not the penalty of Adam'.

The penalty of Adam was to be expelled from the Garden of Eden into a corrupt and fallen world. As a result of his experiences in that 'fallen' world (the court) the Duke is, like Jaques – the man whom he frequently seeks out for company – world-weary. But the message of this director's Romantic text is that this display of world-weariness by one with the *power* to control his subjects and the *duty* to exercise that control cannot be shown as a permanent state of mind. His duty is to be part of the social world. Jaques can stay in the forest; the Duke cannot. People like Jaques will always be on the outside, always ultimately alone. But there is something within the Duke's character –the actor identifies it as being the result of the lull in energy and commitment that often accompanies middle age – which urges him to remain in the forest with Jaques. Even at the very end of the play when the lovers are triumphant and all eyes are fixed on the future, we can hear a note of faint pessimism in the Duke's closing lines

> Proceed, proceed. We'll begin these rites
> *As we do trust they'll end*, in true delights.
> (V.4.194–5, my italics)

This director's text has the Duke make a lengthy pause after the departure of Jaques, as if considering long and hard whether or not to go with him. The actor himself stressed the word 'trust' in the second line. The overall effect is briefly but significantly to throw a slight shadow across the brilliance of the scene. There is a real sense of tension in the theatre as if, at the very last, the Duke might spoil the party and the whole thing collapse and end, not in light and optimism, but in darkness and pessimism. Yet the Duke manages to surmount his reluctance to go back into a world that will inevitably bring him face to face with disappointments and disillusionment. Ultimately it is the faith and confidence exemplified by his daughter that convince him the young are right to trust in the future and that he must do so as well. He *must* enter into the world and accept the trials that being fully human and connected to other people entail. This is, or so it seems to the director and to his cast, a play that urges its audience not to run away to some fantasy utopia but to use fantasy in order to be a part of the real world. To escape the pressures of the real world and to seek renewal in the holiday world can be beneficial, but

> If all the year were playing holidays,
> To sport would be as tedious as to work
> (*1 Henry IV* I.2.199–200)

In discussion, the example of Prospero in *The Tempest* often comes up as an appropriate parallel to Duke Senior. He too is betrayed by a brother. Prospero seems to know at the end of the play that his *duty* is to break his staff, burn his book and leave the island paradise with his daughter and son-in-law to start afresh a new generation back in the old world.

The director hopes that by the end of his *As You Like It* it will be clear to audiences that, in one sense at least, Jaques is correct. The Duke is right in suspecting human motives in the world of the court; his own history of betrayal proves the point. Human beings are capable of cruel and irrational behaviour, but they are also capable of being transformed and redeemed. Miraculous though it may seem it *does* happen:

JAQUES DE BOYS
> Duke Frederick, hearing how that every day
> Men of great worth resorted to this forest,
> Addressed a mighty power, which were on foot,
> In his own conduct, purposely to take
> His brother here and put him to the sword;
> And to the skirts of this wild wood he came,
> Where, meeting with an old religious man,
> After some question with him, was converted
> Both from his enterprise and from the world,
> His crown bequeathing to his banished brother,
> And all their lands restored to them again
> That were with him exiled.

(V.4.151–62)

Of course our director's text has given short shrift to certain ideas and themes undoubtedly present in what Shakespeare wrote. He has also focused almost entirely on three or four characters. It must have been a rather dull experience for whoever was cast as Touchstone! (See Chapter 1 for a more detailed consideration of his role.) For the purposes of this exercise we must assume that time was spent with all the other characters, but for now the director's overall design has been our chief concern.

The Forest of Arden as a holiday world of freedom is certainly how *I* like to think of it. You would be right in pointing out that the forest itself includes wild beasts and snakes that can kill; it is described as a 'desert' peopled by women who are cruel (Phebe), men who suffer for love (Silvius) and false priests (Sir Oliver Martext) who are prepared to sanction a marriage that is palpably unsound (between Touchstone and Audrey). Nevertheless, what we recall in tranquillity is an image of the golden age, or rather the green world; one which for much of the time is covered in snow, but which is transformed to spring with the promise of summer to come. When the imagination looks back and recalls the past it usually excludes memories of days when it rained all day long.

> In spring time, the only pretty ring time,
> When birds do sing, hey ding a ding, ding,
> Sweet lovers love the spring.
>
> (V.3.36–8)

3. A Political Text

Our second director is younger than the first. To date his work has been for 'fringe' companies on low budgets in small theatre spaces. He too is university educated, but not in the tradition of F. R. Leavis. If he acknowledged a mentor, it would probably be Terry Eagleton or Raymond Williams. This young man recalls more of what Karl Marx wrote than of what Helen Gardner said, although he too read English. He is committed to the belief that the role of art is to help raise the consciousness of the working class in order to provoke an analysis that will lead, eventually, to social action. Director number two admires the work of the playwright Bertolt Brecht as much as that of Shakespeare, and has ideological qualms about accepting the offer to direct *As You Like It*. Having done so, he intends to offer a radical challenge to traditional Romantic readings of the text, and to stress that the play is in fact not a simple Romantic comedy, but a complex instrument of social control: a profoundly *political* text with a highly reactionary message.

In Shakespeare criticism, the Romantic interpretation discussed in the preceding chapter can be regarded as the dominant way of reading and producing the play, at least since the nineteenth century. What the young director of our second production asks is whether this interpretation is still valid in the 1980s or 1990s.

His low-budget production is destined to tour the smaller theatres and arts centres outside London. The first rehearsal was called in a dark and cold church hall somewhere in South London. Our director and his designer are somewhat nervously awaiting the arrival of the cast. Fortified by coffee the director at last stands up and addresses the cast. Again, this director is concerned to make what he says appear absolutely spontaneous, in the hope that the cast will be generally impressed and reassured by his eloquence. In fact his detailed commentary is the result of many solitary hours of agonizing preparation (he talks for much longer than our previous director) in which he has decided on what he hopes and believes will be a new striking interpretation of this well-known and well-loved play. He concludes that this very familiarity, or rather the *assumption* made by most audiences and actors that they know the play, has caused it to become theatrically sterile, obscured by layers of historical performance-tradition and sentiment, which has distorted its real meaning. The aim of his production is to make audiences look at the old and familiar material in a new light: to make them re-evaluate and challenge long-held assumptions about the play. The designer (who has been engaged in preliminary discussions and has come to this opening session) is ready to display her model of the set as the director explains his ideas.

I want you to try to forget all the productions of this play that you may have seen in the past. And I especially want you to forget anything you may have been told about it at school.

You must be wondering why I wanted to do this play; why not *Coriolanus* or something more overtly in tune with my interests? Well, I suppose it's because I think that the comedies are generally neglected as vehicles for the transmission of serious ideas about society. There is a widespread assumption amongst many people (including far too many actors and students) that comedy is simply about laughter, and that what makes you laugh or smile is not also intended to make you think. The very title of this play seems to imply a kind of frivolity: it doesn't really matter what the play means; it's up to you to decide, as *you* like it. But in the comedies Shakespeare is making something very serious. He is reproducing a seminal myth of Renaissance culture: the celebration of so-called human individualism. This myth has been at the centre of much Romantic literary criticism. It suggests that individuals can, through their own efforts and personal qualities, meet, challenge and finally overcome all obstacles to personal happiness and fulfilment. Plays such as *As You Like It* do not allow for the defeat of those who are at the centre of the action, and with whom the audience is invited to identify. *As You Like It*'s basic optimism about the human race is based on the assumption that to be personally good, as opposed to evil or corrupt, is in itself sufficient to ensure that there will be a victory for happiness. There is, to be sure, a *threat* to that happiness, but the comedies end with dance, with music and with marriage – all established symbols of harmony, completeness and renewal. Our task is to deconstruct this romantic, fairy-tale view of the world, and to try to make our audience see that beneath the surface of the conventional meanings of the play there is a sub-text which is politically reactionary and deadly serious.

I don't see *As You Like It* as a fairy-tale. I'm tired of seeing it presented in the theatre as bait to catch the tourists; a 'safe' outing to Stratford-on-Avon for favourite sons and daughters of the middle class; dished-up as cultural fodder to be consumed by executives of multinational companies on 'hospitality' jaunts. Did you know that *As You Like It* has been performed at Stratford more often than almost any other play by Shakespeare? It must have at least a fighting chance of being the most performed play ever!

I wish we could give it another title. *As You Like It* sounds so cosy and suffocatingly patronizing. It seems to promise a cloyingly sweet story with a conventional happy ending, and this creates problems for us because audiences will approach what we have prepared for them with preconceived ideas. They are used to productions which confirm their lazy acceptance that, put in the fatalistic language of cliché, in the end everything in life generally works out for the best; when it doesn't there is really nothing to be done to remedy the situation.

Have you ever considered why Shakespeare is apparently so popular? He is after all a compulsory part of almost any humanities education beyond the age of sixteen. We have a huge (and expensive) national theatre company named after him – the only one to bear the epithet 'Royal' on its letter heading. William Shakespeare has become a kind of cultural monument: his face even looks out at the lucky holders of large-denomination bank notes![17] His work is the focus for a vast literary critical industry with branches in higher education and in publishing. Shakespeare's writing is celebrated and seen as a touchstone for quality throughout the western world. It seems to me that the popularity and indeed the growth of the huge Shakespeare industry is in direct proportion to the extent that the plays are considered politically neutral and therefore 'safe'. It is supposed and implicitly stated in some nineteenth-century and much twentieth-century criticism that the comedies, at least, are almost all concerned not to undermine or question an essentially apolitical, static and passive view of the world: one that our political masters past and present would have the populace hold as absolute truth. But I maintain they *are* political, and it is of the essence that in our production the politics of *As You Like It* and the ideology that underpins them are made manifest.

In our work together on this text we must get rid of any thoughts that might perpetuate another myth, i.e. that Shakespeare had some special and unique insight into what has been called the 'human condition' – insight which reveals permanent truths that transcend historical time and are as relevant today as they were in Elizabethan/Jacobean England. We must acknowledge that the so-called human condition is not in itself an absolute state implying something permanent. Shakespeare is not 'for all time'. He does not tell us *the* truth about ourselves. His plays demonstrate, or rather his plays are conventionally produced in order to demonstrate, something that is not value-free, but *a* vision, *a* truth about human society and relationships, seen, inevitably, from a deeply subjective point of view. But it is a view conventionally presented and celebrated as *truth*, not as *fiction*. Instead of encouraging the questioning of social reality the comedies, so presented, encourage passive acceptance of it. The mind is numbed into an acceptance of the general myth expressed as *All's Well That Ends Well*. This is what we must avoid.

To the question 'Why did Shakespeare celebrate stability and the existing order?' the answers are legion. Not least of these must be the desire not to offend the censors or the monarch. But as far as I'm concerned there is an obvious dominating factor: Shakespeare was first and foremost a businessman who successfully made money out of the theatre. What businessmen want, what they *need* to make money in an emerging capitalist system, is order. Disorder is bad news for business; prolonged disorder is catastrophic! Everything Shakespeare wrote into this play supported the contemporary status quo. There is a lot of talk in *As You Like It* about nature and the natural world of Arden (I'd like you to remember that Arden sounds very like Eden) as opposed to the world of the court. What is presented in the play as *natural* is associated with what is also presented as being inherently *good*. The underlying message, the sub-text that Shakespeare intended for his audience, is that to accept without question the given hierarchy of power is natural and therefore good, and to question it or dissent from it is unnatural and therefore bad.

This preoccupation with preserving the existing hierarchical structure, and in the process legitimizing the hegemony, echoes the dominant ideological resistance to change manifested in a variety of official and semi-official utterances during this period. As students of ideology have observed, the more rigorously a set of values is publicly supported, the more likely it is to be under pressure. Thus we need to be alert to reported arguments and the causes which generated them. For instance

Queen Elizabeth I had no heirs and was ageing fast; the orderly transition of power became an overriding concern. Shakespeare's passages about order and succession recapitulate arguments such as those found in the 1559 'Exhortation concerning good order and obedience to rulers and magistrates', which was to be read in all churches and which I'm now going to read to you:

Almighty God hath created and appointed all things in heaven, earth and waters, in a most excellent and perfect order . . . Every degree of people in their vocation, calling, and office hath appointed to them, their duty and order. Some are in high degree, some in low, some kings and princes, some inferiors and subjects, priests and laymen, Masters and Servants, Fathers and children, husbands and wives, rich and poor, and everyone have need of other: So that in all things is to be lauded and praised the goodly order of God, without the which, no house, no city, no commonwealth, can continue and endure or last. For where there is no right order, there reigneth all abuse, carnal liberty, sin, and Babilonicall confusion.

As you probably know, the Elizabethan/Jacobean social structure was strictly hierarchical – think of it as a pyramid. This model is not unlike our own of course, although those at the top are now perhaps less easy to pick out and isolate. But the pyramid is not simply an image of a social structure; it is fundamentally a model of power. In the sixteenth-century schema, the monarch was placed at the top and under her, in descending order, her blood relations, the noble land-owning families of England, the merchants, the yeomen and finally the great mass of the people who owned no property and sold their labour in order to survive precariously within the system. Mobility within this model was virtually nil. The system of power and social control was legitimized through association with the so-called heavenly hierarchy which it was supposed to mirror. The authority of the earthly model was at least in part derived from linking it to that of heaven, and from making the supreme temporal ruler, the monarch, God's representative on earth, appointed to rule by divine decree; ultimately, therefore, he or she carried the weight of a transcendental authority. The earthly kingdom, reflecting dimly the perfect order of heaven, was, if you like, one of the dominant political myths of Elizabethan England.

Those in power, or those like Shakespeare who benefited from a continuance of the status quo, recognized it as a myth, but sought to perpetuate and strengthen it. Shakespeare's plays embody myths: social fictions which form part of a whole web of ideology that is created by art, politics and religion to control the way in which ordinary people see the world and their own position in it. Indeed politicians were constantly on the look out for ways of augmenting the mythology that supported and upheld their claim to power. For example, shortly after attaining power, the house of Tudor (of whom Queen Elizabeth I was the last in line) established an energetic official search for their ancestors. The search 'proved', conveniently enough, that the Tudor line went back to that emotionally powerful mythical English hero, King Arthur, which helped the Tudors. Remember, ideas are powerful. In a society like that into which our national poet was born, social control was maintained without the benefit of a standing army and with no police or paramilitary force of any significant kind. Nothing changed for the vast majority, despite appalling and apparent inequalities of wealth, because the consciousness of the world held by the majority was *controlled* by the myths or the ideology of the minority; it was a false consciousness.

The problem for anyone who today, or at any time in history, seeks to engineer radical social change is this same kind of 'false consciousness'. That is to say that in a capitalist state the masses do not see the world as it is. Instead they are tricked into believing in a fiction of what the world is like; a fiction deliberately created and sustained by the ruling class. *As You Like It* is a tiny but significant part of that fiction. As I have said, it implies that an acceptance of the given hierarchy of power is natural and therefore good and to question it unnatural and therefore bad. Marx taught that in order to change anything fiction must be challenged:

... economic and social processes must not be presented as 'natural', i.e. unalterable and fated, externals no individual can escape, but rather as produced by people and capable of being modified and changed by people.[18]

In Elizabethan England, order was maintained precisely because the majority accepted that the privileges of the few were the result of natural and unalterable forces. It is not physical force that ultimately prevents widespread social change, although, as we know from recent experience, such force is used by the State from time to time to assert its authority. However the basis on which authority rests cannot and will not give way whilst there is widespread and general acceptance of the ideology of the ruling class. This structure is encapsulated in a well-known nineteenth-century hymn (refreshingly directly, modern editions of *Hymns Ancient and Modern*, leave out the verse):

> The rich man in his castle.
> The poor man at his gate,
> God made them high or lowly,
> And ordered their estate.[19]

Thus the fiction goes that if God, and not Man, is ultimately responsible for the organization of society there is nothing that can (or should) be done to change what in any case is fated and unalterable.

Of course *As You Like It* is not an overtly political play, but that is partly why it is so effective in transmitting a far from value-free political message. At the root of its covert propaganda lies the implicit assumption that there *is* such a thing as natural or normal behaviour, and it consists in the passive acceptance of the given social order. This order is both God-given *and* the natural state of man in society. In order to sustain this fiction as an active social myth there must be acceptance of the existence of a time in the past when *all* human behaviour was natural, together with a belief that this time has been lost. Thus in the Bible we can read of a supposedly pre-social world: the Garden of Eden. In that garden Adam and Eve were at first happy and contented with their lot because they never questioned it. Once they had eaten from the tree of knowledge they began to question. God expelled them for disobedience, but the expulsion from paradise was taken to mean that questioning the God-given world is unnatural and bad, although inevitable. Therefore the first instance of such questioning in recorded history (remember in Shakespeare's time the Bible was taken by most people as historical fact) led to a loss of the innocence and happiness which once existed in the pre-social world of Eden.

If you translate the biblical myth into political terms – and this, I suggest, is what *As You Like It* does – then the play becomes a statement about the vital importance of accepting the given power structure, and a warning that deviation from it can lead to chaos rather than enlightenment.

Oliver and Duke Frederick are like Eve. They question and disrupt the given order of the world as they inherited it. It takes a visit back into the natural world of Arden/Eden to remind Duke Frederick, Oliver and the audience of what natural behaviour should be. In Arden, the penalty of Adam is not yet felt. Here men are in touch with a world that existed before the challenge to authority that led to the fall. In this environment love, not hatred or envy, is the dominant force, and it is the benign power of love that turns all (or almost all) in the Forest of Arden back towards the social world. They turn back refreshed, rejuvenated by their encounter with the truths they have rediscovered there. The departure to the real world of the court is not enacted, thus allowing the golden light of the final scene to colour the audience's imagination of the return. If this illuminated ending is to work, the spectators must be made to relax and feel there is no need for them to take action: they would be irresponsible to do so and, more importantly, they have seen their leaders symbolically instructed in the necessity of proper government. The status quo prevails, cosmetically rejuvenated, but essentially unchanged.

After this lengthy speech many in the cast are looking somewhat glazed and anxious. Although one or two of them have been muttering approving noises, most feel slightly uneasy about the forthcoming rehearsal period. This is especially true of the actress chosen to play Rosalind. Despite having worked with the director before and knowing something of his political leanings, she had harboured a hope that in *As You Like It* the traditional focus on the wit and charm of her character would provide the fulcrum on which the action would delicately and delightfully balance. Her dilemma nicely illustrates the fact that in the modern theatre the aims of the director and the cast do not necessarily correspond. This director is concerned with presenting an *interpretation* of the text which will reflect well on his ability to draw out, or squeeze out, meaning previously obscured.

In this production the director decides to begin and end the action with formal and elaborate dances. These additions to the printed text are meant to provide emblems of a well-ordered State and, by modelling the closing dance closely on that which introduces the play, he hopes to suggest to the audience that the return of the court in exile is *not* the beginning of a new era, but the re-establishment of the old order. The validity of this decision may cause the reader to question how truly this production reflects Shakespeare's intention as it appears in the printed text. That text opens not with an image of order but with the threat of disorder and dislocation. The talk and the action of the first minutes of playing time are of a world in conflict, not with an external aggressor, but with itself. Brother is pitted against brother, and those with power seem almost entirely to lack any sense of the need to exercise it with responsibility. It soon becomes apparent that Oliver, the eldest of three brothers, has, according to the custom of seventeenth-century England, inherited the ownership and control of his late father's wealth, and is failing in his obligations to his youngest sibling. This then is the opportunity for Shakespeare to present his first ideological lesson. The practice of inheritance-rights has to be shown and generally acknowledged as ideologically as well as practically legitimate. Thus it is vital for the individual who inherits privilege – through the accident of birth (the natural tie) – to be *seen* to be using that wealth and power in responsible ways. The first son of old Sir Rowland de Boys breaks this principle, and in doing so threatens the unwritten law that upholds the power and control of others of his class and, ultimately, the monarch. He must not be seen to get away with it.

Oliver has not played the game according to rules established by precedent over hundreds of years. In Shakespeare's England the principle and practice of accepting the legitimacy of inherited wealth could only be sustained if the principle of legitimacy were not subverted from within by the abuse of what was understood as natural justice, upon which the claim rested. Rights and privileges must be seen to entail duties and obligations. The dislocation of this principle is the first thing the audience learns when they hear Orlando talking to Adam. They hear of a brother who has been 'charged' by his father to act responsibly (and by implication naturally) towards his brothers. He has sworn to do so and has therefore received the blessing and sanction of his new material and social position from the dying father. The blessing serves to indicate the legitimacy of the smooth transfer of power from one generation to the next. But Oliver abuses his new authority by denying his younger brother *his* birthright. This, as Orlando knows, goes against the unwritten code on which the privileges of the few and the order of the State as a whole are founded:

ORLANDO . . . I know you are my eldest brother, and in the gentle condition of blood you should so know me. The courtesy of nations allows you my better, in that you are the first born, but the same tradition takes not away my blood . . .

(I.1.41–5)

It is *tradition* ('old custom'), not written law, which enshrines and protects the structure of this society. There was, of course, no written constitution in Elizabethan England (we still do not have one today), so the law of the land was established through precedent. Shakespeare, this director is concerned to prove, was writing a subtle propaganda play in as much as he sought to emphasize in the action of *As You Like It* that the consequence of any deviation from established practice of inheritance at any social level must be shown, as indeed it eventually is in the play, as unnatural, undesirable and ultimately untenable.

But before an audience can be expected to recognize and accept that the restoration of the old order is a positive thing it must be made to experience and acknowledge that what preceded it and threatened it was inferior in every way. Thus in the rehearsals for this political production perhaps the most time is spent working on a single powerful and dramatically complex image of dislocation: the wrestling match between Charles and Orlando. This takes place in the first scene, where the whole of the court is on display to the audience. Their sport is emblematic of their conduct.

The contest comes as an interruption of the verbal combat between Rosalind and Celia. Their word-play harmlessly defuses aggression, but the entrance of Le Beau signals the start of a very much more serious form of battle. He tells of an old man whose three sons came to challenge Charles. Their contest, the audience learns, has been no simple demonstration of skill with rules controlling and governing its execution. Instead it was a violent, brutal confrontation: a fight rather than a sporting contest, in which the three sons have been badly hurt. The audience is reminded of the true nature of this 'sport':

TOUCHSTONE It is the first time that ever I heard breaking of ribs was sport for ladies.

(I.2.128–9)

Our director is convinced that the fight between Orlando and Charles must be for real and not a mock combat. He casts both roles in order to emphasize that this is a trial of overwhelming natural physical strength (Charles) versus someone clearly his physical inferior. How then must Orlando's victory be understood by the audience in a political performance-text? Orlando wins, our director tells the cast, because ideologically he *must* win; his defeat would open up the possible interpretation that might could be right. Charles may have natural power but he cannot be shown to have natural authority. Politically the idea of the survival of the strongest is unthinkable. The masses of the people *do* have the potential power to seize control of their own collective destiny; that they have not seized it was, and is, according to our director, *because they are controlled by an ideology which persuades them that they are not fit to hold it*. Orlando wins, not because he is physically more powerful than Charles, but because he can and does use his natural intelligence to out-wit and out-manoeuvre his opponent. Despite all appearances, he is still the *natural superior* to Charles. It is a crucial incident in a political reading of the play, for the audience's expectation is confounded. Their eyes tell them that Charles should win; his reputation that he must. Unlike Orlando, Charles, the wrestler, is not born into the ruling class, and his defeat serves to suggest to those who witness it that it is foolish to try matching strength against natural masters. The message is clear: class (or blood) prevails, not through brute strength, but because nature intended it so. Orlando is *born* to control others who are only superficially his natural superiors.

This idea of the inner or natural superiority of the ruling class is very important in this production of the play, as indeed Rosalind demonstrates when she falls in love with Orlando before knowing that his birth is compatible with her own. She knows that superiority is recognizable, despite external appearances. Similarly when Oliver falls in love with Celia, whom he thinks a simple shepherdess, he is prepared to remain with her in the forest because he knows that such an alliance would be unthinkable in the social world of the court. The reader or spectator knows that the evidence of eyes is not to be trusted; it is Oliver's natural ability to recognize one of his own kind that is proved true. The same thing happens in *The Winter's Tale*. There Perdita, although born into the very highest stratum of society (her father is a king, her mother a queen), is abandoned as a baby in a foreign country and raised by a shepherd as his own daughter. To the young Prince Florizel, who discovers her, Perdita looks what she is not – a simple shepherdess – and yet despite the gap in their apparent social positions, he cannot prevent himself from falling in love. His father, when he appears on the scene, will hear nothing of the proposed marriage; it goes against the whole basis on which his society (and that of Shakespeare) was founded. Only after the revelation of Perdita's natural parentage can the match be condoned and the marriage celebrated. The point is that Florizel, like Rosalind and Oliver, is able to recognize the supposed *natural* superiority of the woman he loves.

We can, I think, agree with the director that Oliver is not the only brother in this tale whose behaviour challenges the ideology underpinning Elizabethan social life, because the action that reveals Oliver's anti-social behaviour also reveals the very unbrotherly and also, by implication, unnatural doings of Duke Frederick. The audience learns that at some time in the past, but a time none the less close enough to remain the subject of current gossip at court, the 'old Duke is banished by his younger brother the new Duke' (I.1.94–5). As in the case of Oliver and Orlando, this is a dislocation of what ought, as far as Shakespeare and most of his contemporaries were concerned, to be recognized as the proper and natural order of things. An older brother depriving a younger of his rights, and a younger denying an older his, turns the Elizabethan ideal of an ordered world on its head. Any society is threatened with collapse into anarchy if the orderly transfer of power from one generation to another is broken up or disrupted. Shakespeare, therefore, does not allow the younger Duke or the elder brother to be seen to be getting away with such aberrant behaviour. The enactment of the subsequent text shows Duke Frederick and Oliver to be both wrong in practice and principle: both are behaving unnaturally.

As we have already noted, meaning is manufactured during performance by an audience listening to a spoken text whilst at the same time observing the context in which those words are heard and said. Therefore in any theatrical reading of a play an important area for consideration must be the design of the production. This includes setting, costumes, lighting and sound as well as the grouping of the actors on the stage. By studying the co-operation between designer and director, it is possible to see the way in which meaning in a play can be manufactured visually. This emphasizes the need for a student reading any play to develop a careful and detailed idea of the way in which his or her imaginary production looks and works. For instance, the designer and director in this hypothetical 'political' production decide to make the forest setting look deliberately artificial by employing cardboard cut-out trees and painted backcloths. By contrast the scenes at court are set realistically. It is also decided to update the action to the 1930s and for the architecture of the court to resemble that beloved of European fascist dictators. A sense of space is created by exaggerating height and depth, and much use is made of cool marble enlivened with splashes of colour provided by hanging flags bearing the emblem of Duke Frederick's court. Furniture is sparse, designed to impress rather than comfort the visitor. Women in the cast are forbidden to rehearse in trousers and instead wear long, tight, movement-restricting skirts. The costumes worn in the eventual production are the period-equivalent of Renaissance court dress. The men of the court wear military costumes – full of braid and medals, beautifully cut and tailored; the women are always elegantly and formally dressed in costumes that restrict their natural movement. All the costumes and the setting of the court in which they are to be seen are intended to *display* power and to distinguish those who have it from those who do not. The director's point is that the ruling class need to contrive elaborate codes of social behaviour in order to provide external evidence of their supposed inner, natural superiority. Thus Rosalind and Celia are given high collars, which force them into very upright stances and restrain their neck and head movements. Their long, tightly waisted robes make them appear like moving pieces of almost-solid sculpture. In fact, the idea for the constricting collars is adopted from earlier Hayden Griffin designs (*As You Like It*, National Theatre, 1979, directed by John Dexter), in which costume had been used visually to emphasize the distinction between the world of leisure (the court) and the world of work (the world of Adam and, at the outset, of Orlando).

But in the forest scenes of our political text costumes *continue* to be used visually to reinforce the social hierarchy. When Rosalind and Celia are first seen in Arden the director stresses to both actors that they are to demonstrate by their actions that neither character could or would unlearn the behaviour previously shown in the court. They still, he argues, have a need to establish their superiority over the likes of Corin and Silvius. Indeed the director stresses that Rosalind's disguise does not and should not cover the aristocratic swagger with which she confidently commands and orders the behaviour of her social inferiors – in particular that of Silvius and Phebe in Act III scene 5. This is another critical point in this director's reading of the play: as far as he is concerned, nothing really changes in the Forest of Arden. The same power structure exists even in paradise!

Addressing those actors who are to play courtiers, both in the court itself and in the Forest of Arden, our director tells them:

The manner of the courtiers does alter with their circumstances, but, do remember that none the less it still successfully sets them apart from their social inferiors. They are dressed as 'outlaws and foresters', not as shepherds and shepherdesses. Duke Senior is still recognizably the centre of power in the forest but his command, unlike that of his younger brother, is supposedly legitimized because, of their own volition and not through coercion, his followers recognize him as their leader and superior. Duke Senior cannot offer material rewards, yet his authority commands allegiance because it is perceived as natural. In the famous opening speech of the second Act, when the audience see the banished court for the first time, Duke Senior stresses the naturalness of their life (and therefore, of course, the way in which that life is organized) in comparison to the 'fallen' world of the court of Duke Frederick:

DUKE

    Now my co-mates and brothers in exile,
    Hath not old custom made this life more sweet
    Than that of painted pomp? Are not these woods
    More free from peril than the envious court?
    Here feel we not the penalty of Adam . . .

                    (II.1.1–5)

In Arden, according to the Duke, there are none of the trappings of the 'painted', i.e. artificial and disguised, behaviour associated with the old life at court and with the social world. In Arden there is no point in simply sweating for advancement; there is nowhere to advance to unless it be towards the affection of the Duke himself. Virtue here is its own reward. The Duke is like a magnet to those merry men who, living according to the values of a past golden age recreated in this magical and mythical place, are designed to show how life should be lived. You cannot, Shakespeare tells us, get back to a non-material, pre-social world; you cannot regain the Garden of Eden, but you *ought* to respect and aspire towards non-material values and ultimately that means an acceptance of your given station in life.

The contrast between our imagined production's use of the forest scenes and the textual emphasis on the natural virtue and authority of the exiled court establishes an interesting dialectic. The audience hears one thing yet is visually reminded of another: the Duke may have 'natural' authority and right to rule, but at the moment he can only exercise it in a pastoral kingdom – a point brought home in production by the highly contrived forest settings. There can be no confusing Arden for reality in this production. The real world has rejected what the text informs us is the right and proper order of social life.

When striving to create strong visual ways in which to stimulate such a complex counterpoint between what is said and what is seen, a director frequently employs rehearsal techniques which help the cast to make them clear. This preparation is particularly important when trying to convey discourses which are unwritten but nevertheless inscribed in a play. Often what is discovered during rehearsals greatly influences the finished production. Therefore let us imagine some of the exercises our director may devise to help his actors provoke the response he is seeking.

To begin with there is a lot of improvisation at the early rehearsals. This focuses on the set of characters who have to behave in a very formal way towards each other. Making the formality meaningful takes considerable effort and thought. An Elizabethan/Jacobean audience would have expected the ritual and pageantry of the court to be accurate, and would have been accustomed to interpreting what they saw. This director has to prepare his actors so that they can convey a kind of formal behaviour which a present-day audience can interpret equally well. Games are developed in which couples have to discover ways of communicating their social ranking. When working, not only on the court scenes, but also on those set in the forest, the director urges the cast always to remember that, like their costumes, their behaviour towards one another is a *display*, played out as if on a public stage where performance is judged, and poor results punished by a lesser role or even banishment from the 'play' altogether. The actors have to be capable of demonstrating to the audience, through gesture and posture as well as through the spoken text, that to be a part of this court is to inhabit a world that requires its subjects to acquire and display an elaborate and restricted code of behaviour. Those capable of mastering this code and correctly enacting its accompanying rituals are demonstrating that they are naturally suited for power.

Our director is well aware that *As You Like It* was written at a time of anxiety about the smooth transfer of power from a long-established order to one which was entirely unknown. For this reason he thinks it highly significant that Shakespeare opens the play by raising questions about power, privilege and responsibility. And to a large extent he is right; *As You Like It* does show the audience people in possession of power who are abusing it. Oliver has abused an important principle, and Duke Frederick has clearly flouted the traditional rights of his elder brother – rights which are a fundamental part of the fabric of Elizabethan society. Their behaviour must therefore be shown – if the aim is to preserve that society – as deviant. Shakespeare accordingly makes both men subject to irrational (i.e. unnatural) outbursts; how could rational-thinking individuals be seen to take such actions? For example, Oliver has, we learn, behaved perfectly properly towards his other brother Jaques, whom he has sent away to be educated, yet he neglects to do the same for Orlando, whom he hates. His hatred is never explained; indeed, he confesses to himself (and to the audience) that 'I hope I shall see an end of him, for my soul – yet I know not why – hates nothing more than he' (I.1.153–4). Similarly the Duke's reaction towards Rosalind – whom, we have previously been informed, he has loved as a daughter since childhood – is wild and almost out of control. It surges through him like an illness and infects his natural feelings towards his own daughter, distorting them and forcing a break-up of their relationship. All this behaviour is juxtaposed with the very positive and, by implication, natural feelings expressed by two other blood-relations: Celia and Rosalind. They demonstrate how people ideally ought to behave towards one another. As Le Beau says, their tie is even 'dearer than the natural bond of sisters':

CELIA
   . . . we still have slept together,
  Rose at an instant, learned, played, eat together
  And whereso'er we went, like Juno's swans
  Still we went coupled and inseparable.
                (I.3.71–4)

Whether or not this production is attractive to an audience or entirely faithful to Shakespeare's text is arguable. Our director is certainly correct in at least one respect: the first Act of *As You Like It* has, in the past, received disproportionately little critical attention compared to the rest of the play. There has always been a rush to get into the forest and begin the 'real business' of the play. In making our political performance-text that trend has been reversed, for the court world designed and developed in rehearsals needs to be well-established in performance to provide a sufficiently strong counterpoint to the subsequent portrayal of Arden. The behaviour of Duke Frederick and Oliver suggests the obvious lack of harmony and order that must be present in any stable political state. The audience must understand the consequences of action dictated by individual desire rather than by the responsibilities implicit in *noblesse oblige*, and if they have vicariously experienced the insecurity and unhappiness of such a world, then they will welcome the re-establishment of older, more stable, traditional values all the more.

Adam encapsulates the state of affairs encountered in that first act when he cries:

        O what a world is this, when what is comely
        Envenoms him that bears it!
              (II.3.14–15)

The first Act of *As You Like It* shows a society sick and out of joint. The political identification of the cause centres on the inevitable consequences of disregarding the natural order of society and its government – which is also the existing ideological model. The conclusion is similar to that reached in the Romantic text. There, however, the production and the thinking behind it concentrate on the morality of the characters' behaviour in an essentially Christian context. The political assessment is more pragmatic, being concerned with the way in which events and ideas can be manipulated to preserve the existing power structure. But both agree that the situation is precarious because wrong.

As our present director sees it, Shakespeare's bleak picture of a world in conflict with itself can be shown because at the same time the audience is given enough guidance to see and acknowledge that before the world became as it is now presented to them, it was otherwise, and better, and can be so again. This is a fallen world but the assumption is that the values of the lost golden world can at least be partially regained. The desirability of the old in comparison to the new comes from its supposed stability and inherent fairness, a condition derived from a general acceptance of a presupposed natural order being mirrored in the social order.

How does our director use the text to locate and make this point? He establishes that in the first act there is a lot of talk about what life was like in the past. The first such reference comes from Charles the wrestler when he tells Oliver of the recent history of the expulsion of Duke Senior.

OLIVER Where will the old Duke live?
CHARLES They say he is already in the Forest of Arden, and a many merry men with him; and there they live like the old Robin Hood of England: they say many young gentlemen flock to him every day, and fleet the time carelessly as they did in the golden world.

(I.1.108–12)

This lyrical recalling of a past golden age, and the linking of it to the popular Elizabethan folk hero Robin Hood, is taken further in Orlando's response to Adam's generosity in the second Act. Adam has offered to go with Orlando when he flees his brother's house. In more ordinary circumstances Adam's loyalty would be directed towards the elder brother as the legitimate heir to his old master. But Oliver's actions are grounds enough for Adam's acceptance not of the letter of the law but of the principle of natural justice. The escape of both men is made possible by Adam's practical display of one of the cardinal virtues: thrift. In his outpouring of thanks, Orlando tells how Adam's reactions recall the golden values of an almost forgotten past:

ORLANDO
O good old man, how well in thee appears
The constant service of the antique world,
When service sweat for duty, not for meed!
Thou art not for the fashion of these times,
Where none will sweat but for promotion,
And having that do choke their service up
Even with the having; it is not so with thee.
(II.3.56–62)

This speech can be compared with the dying John of Gaunt's in *Richard II*:

This royal throne of kings, this sceptred isle,
This earth of majesty, this seat of Mars,
This other Eden – demi-paradise –
This fortress built by nature for herself
Against infection and the hand of war,
This happy breed of men, this little world,
This precious stone set in the silver sea . . .
(II.1.40–47)

Both men conjure up images of England's former glories though, significantly, Orlando's eulogy to Adam relies on plebeian virtues (service, sweat, duty) while Gaunt's to his own king uses idealized rhetoric. Both, however, look back to a golden age now threatened with disintegration because of a disregard for the values of the past. In *Richard II* that past is irretrievably lost, but in *As You Like It* the golden world is kept alive in Arden and eventually brought out of the forest and back into the world of the court. History does come full circle; order is restored in a rejuvenated, legitimate court. Brother is reconciled with brother; the rights of the elder are reinstated, and a new generation born to those who have brought about this reformation.

With this resounding 'happy ending', complete with marriages and music, it is tempting to disregard politics. In the kind of production we have been constructing, however, this urge to relax into resolution, harmony and optimism is by its nature worthy of investigation. Did Shakespeare intend it to be plausible? If so, why incorporate so many obviously incongruent elements? (The return of the third son of old Sir Rowland for one.) Effectively a magic wand is waved over the forest and the desolate refuge becomes a fertile bower. All obstacles to love and rightful power dissolve; all wrongs are righted and the young couples seem to promise this state will be perpetuated. It may be that the playwright truly wanted to offer a metaphoric reward for preserving the status quo; this message would have been comfortable and also popular with the Crown. Certainly that is one reading of the play which cannot be denied. However, it can be questioned.

Our political director has been raising questions all along, and if his interpretation works then this ending must be seen, like many of the issues this imaginary production raises, to be sounding a warning note to those in power. What is taking place on stage is the visible creation of a mythology to underpin a government. If mythology can be created, it can also be destroyed, and by accentuating in performance the inconsistencies and improbabilities of the ending, it is possible by suggestion to point to similar weaknesses in the mythological foundation of the dominant ideology. The intention is never to incite rebellion, but to make those in authority realize how much they, like the playwright, depend on the willing suspension of disbelief.

Such a reading does not depend on political insights gained in our own time. The Renaissance was a period of acute political acumen, and much political analysis and debate was published and available to someone of Shakespeare's education and social circle. One of those political commentators, Sir Thomas More, had earlier observed: 'One of the highest achievements of power is to impose fictions upon the world, and one of its supreme pleasures is to enforce the acceptance of fictions that are known to be fictions.'[20] He was not alone in identifying or exposing political practices in Renaissance England, and Shakespeare was likely to have encountered at least some of these ideas. For this director, at least, *As You Like It* is both the retelling of such a propagandist fiction, in order to facilitate social stability by forestalling general apprehension, at a time of transition, of the precarious nature of power, and also a vehicle for political commentary, in that it reveals the means by which the Crown sought to legitimize itself.

A political reading of the play is therefore not necessarily a distortion of the text, although it stresses some aspects of it at the expense of others. The director's opposition of court and forest, real and ideal, artificial and natural, can be said to be a legitimate recognition of the contradictions and paradoxes typical of Renaissance culture. His resulting performance-text, which suggests that the playwright deliberately chooses to support the existing order while simultaneously making clear that he is refraining from demystifying monarchy, may suggest many new and interesting ways of regarding the characters and their actions in this text. Remember that there is a sense in which all literature and art is political. We usually term 'political theatre' plays that offer a specific 'left-wing' analysis and critique of our political system. But you could argue that a play that seems to ignore politics entirely is, none the less, offering at least tacit support for the continuance of the status quo. And that, of course, *is* a political position.

4. A Feminist Text

This third director is the youngest of the three. She is still an undergraduate and intends to direct *As You Like It* in the extensive grounds of her college, using a cast made up of fellow students. In this final imaginary production Rosalind will be played by a sixteen-year-old boy and Celia by a girl, his twin sister.

We will now be looking at a performance-text created by a director who can be described as a feminist in as much as she is interested in literature, art and politics generated *by* women *for* women. Throughout her education this young woman has become increasingly aware that the picture of the world offered for mass consumption by politicians, the media and the arts is one manufactured almost exclusively by men for men. It pretends to some extent that its concerns are universal and transcend questions of sex and gender but, as far as the experience of this particular woman is concerned, this is simply not the case in practice.

In the theatre industry she knows that the production and transmission of plays is almost exclusively controlled by men. It is not that she feels that all men are 'anti-women', or even that some men are not capable of representing women in significant ways, but simply that the distribution of gender in the population as a whole is not reflected in the balance of power and control in the theatre and elsewhere. For example, although her ambition is to work in the professional theatre, she knows that very few women earn their living as directors.[21] Moreover, the power-model in operation in professional theatre reflects a male concern with establishing and sustaining a hierarchy (the director controls and *directs*), which she feels militates against a more co-operative form of organization with which she and others with whom she works are in sympathy. A production in which the director has total artistic control is, she suggests, quintessentially male.

This director has chosen to work on *As You Like It* following lengthy discussions with fellow students who wanted to act in a production but did not want to be *told* what the production should be. The collective decision to work on a play by Shakespeare was partly an acknowledgement that the playwright represents a dominant part of the liberal education of most young people. It was also considered an interesting challenge as currently there are so many unwritten and unspoken assumptions about Shakespeare's work in both the theatre and in literary criticism. For instance it is taken for granted that his plays are significant and intrinsically worthy of the attention they receive. This assumption is based on another: namely that what a man called Shakespeare wrote over four hundred years ago somehow manages to transcend the barriers of time, culture and gender to speak to audiences and readers with a freshness and relevance that defies history. Shakespeare's work, according to the tradition exemplified in the Romantic text, is supposed to embody lasting and permanent values about the 'human condition'. In their discussions this group of students recognized that Shakespeare *is* significant, but they also knew that what his work signifies is connected to the production process of his plays in the theatre and the current cultural interpretation *given* to that process.

As You Like It was originally suggested as a possible piece on which to work because it appeared to offer at least one tremendous role for a woman, and seemed to be concerned with a woman who controlled the affairs of men rather than being herself subject to male domination. Rosalind seemed to be a female heroine; a woman liberated by disguise from the restricting conventions of her society and culture; an example of what women could be if they were free from male constraints. But this view did not survive long once discussion, analysis and rehearsal took over.

There was no opening speech from the director to the assembled cast. However she later wrote an article based on the production, which was published shortly after she graduated. It is from this I quote:

Critical Studies: As You Like It

The persistent claims for the universality of Shakespeare's appeal to audiences and readers has, I think, at the very least to be questioned by both women *and* men. The products of the Elizabethan and Jacobean theatre industry were staged in theatres owned and operated exclusively by men. There were no women actors, stage-hands or shareholders. Although women attended the plays, they comprised only a small section of the audience, and often their presence was discouraged. To understand Shakespeare it is necessary to read him in the context of history and, in particular, the history of theatrical convention that governed the production and presentation of plays such as *As You Like It*.

Shakespeare's theatre practice, like that of his contemporaries, was not illusionistic. That is to say, no attempt was made to convince an audience that they were witnessing reality on stage. Geographical locations could be defined by the spoken text as in *Twelfth Night*, when Viola asks 'What country, friends, is this?' and the Captain replies 'This is Illyria, Lady' (I.2.1–2). Simple representational scenery could also be used. Although a construction such as a 'tree', made out of canvas and wood, might be used to represent, say, the Forest of Arden, that tree would be there to *represent* a real location rather than attempting, at any level, to encourage the audience in the belief that it *was* the thing it represented.

Likewise in acting, despite Hamlet's advice to the players to

Suit the action to the word, the word to the action, with this special observance, that you o'erstep not the modesty of nature. For anything so o'erdone is from the purpose of playing, whose end, both at the first and now, was and is to hold, as 'twere, the mirror up to nature . . .

(*Hamlet* III.2.18–23)

it is very unlikely indeed that the Elizabethan actors approached their roles in what we would now recognize and term a naturalistic style. The technique of submerging the personality of the actor and taking on that of the character, in a manner advocated by Stanislavski at the end of the nineteenth century, would have been almost impossible to achieve in the conditions experienced by Elizabethan players.[22] To start with, the actor's knowledge and experience of the play was often limited to his time on stage. Each had only a copy of his part (or parts) with exits and entrances marked. One of the reasons for this was to prevent plays being sold to rival companies; it also saved on the time and cost of providing each member of the company with a complete text of the whole play. Detailed study of the text as a whole, therefore, would have been impossible.

Rehearsal conditions also prevented any extensive exploration of character – exploration essential to effective naturalistic performance. Plays had minimal rehearsal time and, in any case, such rehearsal would not have concerned itself with the presentational strategy behind a particular 'reading' of the dramatist's text. A few days were all that the Elizabethans could usually afford – this in comparison to the four to six weeks taken by most established companies today.

This contrast in approach is significant, for actors, directors, designers, audiences and readers are all, in a sense, prisoners of history. When looking at dramatic texts in order to discover their theatrical potential we all are influenced by echoes of past performances and previous readings. We cannot read *As You Like It* (or any other play) in a theatrical vacuum. The text becomes the product of our individual experiences of the theatre: experiences gained at either first or second hand. Such experience has been moulded by a predominantly naturalistic convention in the acting and, to a lesser extent, the staging of classic drama. Much critical thinking about Shakespeare has until very recently approached the text and its subsequent animation in the mind's eye with eyes and ears attuned to the theatre language of naturalistic acting and representational staging.[23] This perspective, although valid enough in its own terms, is not the only one open to scholars or to theatre practitioners. What follows from it has often been a rather lazy acceptance of at least two common assumptions about Shakespeare. First, that boy actors were *only* used to play women because women were not available as actors and second, that audiences had to 'suspend their disbelief' when watching boys enact women in order to collude in the manufacture of significant 'female' roles. In plays like *Twelfth Night* and *As You Like It*, where cross-dressing is so significant a feature, I think Shakespeare wanted his audience to see Viola/Cesario and Rosalind/Ganymede not as exclusively female, but as being inseparable from the actor with distinct and recognizable *male* qualities.

Given the non-representational staging and the rehearsal conditions governing the subsequent enactment of the text, it is certainly arguable that the first audiences for *As You Like It* were always aware of the true gender of the 'women' they watched. By extension it is possible to suggest that this is precisely what Shakespeare wanted. The case of Rosalind/Ganymede supports such a reading, for, as I shall attempt to show, the dual sexuality is made a feature of in the text in performance. It is difficult for a generation raised on the experience and memory of seeing the likes of Edith Evans, Vanessa Redgrave and Kate Nelligan to bear in mind that originally the role was played by a young man, to a largely male audience *knowing* him to be male. As a consequence, what we see today – in the theatre or in our imagination – when Ganymede is on stage is a woman thinly disguised as male; the opposite, I suggest, of what Shakespeare intended. This is one of the central ideas our group explored in rehearsals. Its significance was made more apparent during our research into past productions of the play.

Although Rosalind has always been the principal focus of critical attention, and more recently the role has been perceived as a great opportunity for an *actress*, at least two-thirds of 'her' time on stage is spent impersonating a man. In the past, theatre critics, the vast majority of whom are male, have always been somewhat uneasy about this cross-dressing. Their reviews invariably stress the 'femininity' of Ganymede; not any masculine qualities that may or may not have been revealed or brought to the role. Indeed, judging from reviews it would seem that when taking on the part actresses themselves have never at any time during their performance seriously attempted to convince an audience that they are anything other than female. The dressing-up is played as a charade, not as a serious attempt at male impersonation. From Mrs Siddons onwards (she incidentally was too modest to wear breeches for Ganymede and instead wore an 'ambiguous vestment, that seemed neither male nor female'),[24] favourite critical adjectives for describing performances have been 'grace', 'charm', 'feminine' and 'womanly'. A fairly typical example is provided by Clement Scott, theatre critic of the *Herald*, writing about the performance of Ada Rehan in London during the summer of 1897. Scott is almost desperate to prove to his readers (and to himself?) that there had been no impropriety in a performance he so obviously relished and which, it seems, his subconscious was telling him was just a little improper:

Her Rosalind has three distinct qualities – grace, humour, and womanliness ... The great feature of Miss Rehan's Rosalind is that she never for one moment forgets that she is a woman ... the very instant she is left alone with Celia she beomes a woman again to the very finger-tips, kissing and clasping and embracing her sister, for very reaction, after all this pent-up excitement. She enters into the masquerade with the recklessness of high spirits, and in the high spirits of a girl dressed up as a boy there must be some excess. But excessive or not, strained possibility now and then to too high a pitch; there is not an atom of vulgarity in Miss Rehan's Rosalind. She may let her high spirits run away with her, but she is always a woman, always graceful, always with a reserve of dignity to fall back upon. Wild and impulsive she may be, but always refined. The charm of the new Rosalind is that she is a woman. She is no tomboy, or hoyden, or heavy lump of humanity – she is womanly.

Scott's review and his notion of what characterized an attractive and appropriate Rosalind encapsulate the extent to which critical practice, at least since the nineteenth century, has emphasized the female side of Rosalind's character. The convention of the boy-actor was lost in the focus on the girl playing the part of a boy. This distorts the theatre conditions for which Shakespeare wrote, and though he may well have been interested in exploring aspects of femininity he would not have forgotten that a woman would never be speaking the lines in his theatre. One member of our collective was particularly interested in feminist linguistics and it was she who convinced the rest of us that Shakespeare was indeed not writing lines for a woman, or supporting female equality – a reading now frequently imposed on the play. Those modern critics who advocate the theories of Lacan and Kristeva argue that our concepts of what constitutes masculinity and femininity are ordered *not* by biological considerations but by language.[25] At no point, she argued, does Shakespeare write what such critics would recognize as 'feminine' dialogue for Rosalind. These critics have asserted that what traditionally is made to characterize feminine discourse is irrationality, chaos and fragmentation. But Rosalind's text is characteristically male. It is reasoned, ordered, unified and lucid. However, gender as determined by language is always regarded as unstable and shifting; masculine rationality, for instance, is always subject to fissures by insertions of irrational, fragmentary speech. You can see this happening after Rosalind/Ganymede hears of the wounding of Orlando in Act IV scene 3.

In the character of Rosalind Shakespeare provides a de-stabilized representation of gender by causing 'her' to move through different sexual identities as she takes on and then abandons the Ganymede disguise. The character appears to shift from female to male and back to female. The Rosalind/Ganymede role is further disrupted by the knowledge that the actor playing both parts is male. Thus he moves from male actor to female role, to male role and back to female role, never completely losing his actual male self. Despite the visual instability, however, the Rosalind/Ganymede spoken text is almost entirely masculine. The character is ruled by reason (even her falling in love is controlled, for she doesn't let Orlando know that she reciprocates his passion until she has schooled him to a social level which makes him acceptable to her).

The scenes between Rosalind/Ganymede and Orlando always show Rosalind as Orlando's equal or better – until the final scene of the play when her previous masculinity is entirely subordinated. This would not be the case if she were actually intended to be accepted as a woman when seen as Ganymede, for Orlando is in fact her social equal and a male and therefore it is *he* who should be dominant in each encounter. Instead, their sexual/social ordering is inverted: it is Orlando who is ruled by passion and it is his discourse, especially as represented by the poems to his love, that is fragmentary and incoherent.

In the dramatic life of this period any female character who does not conform to the male ideal of woman is suspect. Any woman who displays an independence of men is eventually either destroyed (like Lady Macbeth) or else submits herself finally to male authority (Katherine in *The Taming of the Shrew*). In *As You Like It* the apparent independence shown by Rosalind comes only when she is portraying the male Ganymede. In the following exchange with Orlando it is the *male* actor who is heard *and seen* speculating on the future marriage:

ORLANDO O, but she is wise.

ROSALIND Or else she could not have the wit to do this. The wiser, the way-warder. Make the doors upon a woman's wit, and it will out at the casement; shut that, and 'twill out at the key-hole; stop that, 'twill fly with the smoke out at the chimney.

ORLANDO A man that had a wife with such a wit, he might say 'Wit, wither wilt?'

ROSALIND Nay, you might keep that check for it, till you met your wife's wit going to your neighbour's bed.

ORLANDO And what wit could wit have to excuse that?

ROSALIND Marry, to say she came to seek you there. You shall never take her without her answer, unless you take her without her tongue. O, that woman that cannot make her fault her husband's occasion, let her never nurse her child herself, for she will breed it like a fool.

(IV.1.148–63)

Not surprisingly, these lines form the cue for Orlando to leave the stage, doubtless to reflect on where his desires may end up leading him.

The enactment of the role of Rosalind by a boy-actor entails him in the presentation not of one consistent character who happens to take on a disguise, but in two: Rosalind and Ganymede. If you look carefully at extracts like that above you will agree, I hope, that there are times in the performance when the boy speaks as Rosalind and other times (by far the majority) when he speaks as a man/boy, as Ganymede. Hence the warnings to the young male embroiled in the emotions of courtship can be understood as coming *not* from an enlightened sympathetic female partner, but from one man to another. We can assume, I think, that the actors playing Ganymede and Orlando are much of an age, and therefore what the audience in the theatre sees is a meeting of two young men, both of marriageable age, who sound out a distinct warning about the dangers that surround the married man. Throughout the action of *As You Like It* the movement between representing male and then female gender by the actor reminds the audience that Orlando's need is to subdue and master Rosalind in marriage. Their relationship should not be presented as a romantic partnership of social equals. To see it as such is to take a modern, romantic and distorting view of what is actually taking place on the stage.

The whole area of sexuality becomes interestingly confused and problematic once we re-focus our perceptions and see and hear Ganymede as male – not female thinly disguised as male. In the late-1960s there was a now-famous production of *As You Like It* with an all-male cast. Ronald Pickup played Rosalind and the director was Clifford Williams. It was a production based on what now seems to be a curious set of assumptions:

The examination of the infinite beauty of Man [sic] in love – which lies at the very heart of *As You Like It* – takes place in an atmosphere of spiritual purity, which transcends sensuality in the search for poetic sexuality. It is for this reason that I employ a male cast, so that we shall not – entranced by the surface reality – miss the interior truth.

(From a programme note by Clifford Williams)

'Poetic sexuality'! It seems that Williams was terrified (or perhaps the terror came from his actors) of showing any relationship that could be construed as deviant or homosexual. The use of an all-male cast seems to have been a sub-Brechtian device to distance the audience from its conventional attachment to male/female wooing. But this 'sensuality' that Williams deliberately avoids is, it seemed to us, at the very heart of this play. Whether played by two men or by a man and a woman the courtship of Rosalind and Orlando is undoubtedly sexual. Williams must have entirely ignored Ganymede/Rosalind's statement about the love relationship of Celia and Oliver, where s/he states quite bluntly that the pair are desperate to couple:

. . . they made a pair of stairs to marriage which they will climb incontinent or else be incontinent before marriage.

(V.2.36–8)

Not much 'poetic sexuality' there.

More recently, the RSC production by Terry Hands, which had Susan Fleetwood as Rosalind and John Bowe as Orlando, got much closer to the sensuality that is certainly potentially present in the exchanges between the lovers. In Act IV their love games were seen to shock the silent observer (Celia) when Rosalind, as Orlando makes to leave, rises and 'pretending that she is naked, drops Celia's shawl, which they have been using as a bedspread'.[26] While not seeking to insert gratuitous sexuality into our performance-text, we all agreed that such encounters have a sexual content and are therefore worth examining for what they say about male/female relationships and romantic love – heterosexual or otherwise. They also offer interesting insights into the history of the regulation of sexuality. The fact that when *As You Like It* (and other Shakespeare plays which require cross-dressing and irregular loves) was performed with the encounters played by two men meant that there was freedom to observe and vicariously participate in sexual relationships which have come to be regarded as perverse. Additionally, if both characters are demonstrably male, it opens up the possibilities for a parody of romantic wooing – subverting and undermining the idealization of male/female relationships by emphasizing (through the male partner, Ganymede) a cynical male view of their outcome.

The interpretation of the history of sexuality offered by the critic Foucault suggests that in the eighteenth and nineteenth century the State came to take on the regulation of sexuality as a means of consolidating its power and exercising control.[27] One aspect of this was to highlight the perverse nature of all sex not specifically concerned with reproduction. The endeavour was to 'transform the sexual conduct of couples into a concerted economic and political behaviour',[28] and non-procreative sex therefore came to be regarded as illegitimate. In our discussions we agreed that Foucault's theory could also be applied to *As You Like It*, for although, as I have tried to argue, the conditions of the original performance do show sexual deviance in the overt sexuality of the courtship of two young males, the play none the less ends with the presentation of a conventional male/female union. The affirmation of heterosexual love is the sexually orthodox conclusion of *As You Like It*. But as long as it was acted by an all-male cast sexuality was rendered problematic, and there remained the opportunity for a covert display of homosexuality. When actresses took over the role of Rosalind after the Restoration this discourse was effectively eliminated.

What to us, during the process of rehearsals, became the overtly homosexual nature of the Ganymede/Orlando wooing was subsequently substantiated by some research undertaken by the actor playing Orlando. From his reading of some of the contemporary satirical poetry of the period, in particular Marston's *The Scourge of Villainie*, Middleton's *Micro-cynicon* and John Donne's *Satire 1*, he argued that it was clear that, for these writers at least, homosexuality was regarded as the supreme indulgence of the over-passionate man. He turns to boys and young men because he has exhausted the possibilities of women! Orlando is from the start (and this is how our actor portrayed him) a *virile* and passionate young man. In Arden he is subjected to pressures of extreme emotion, and is so overwhelmed by the forces of sexuality that he turns with enthusiasm to someone whom he believes is a boy. This, we all agreed, is at one and the same time both the satirical presentation of Orlando's excessive lustfulness within a well-established literary tradition and (the point of satire of course) its remedy!

Issues other than cross-dressing and gender also emerged from our reading and rehearsal of *As You Like It*. These again involved a study of the material, literary and political conditions out of which Shakespeare's text evolved.

Elizabethan society was predominantly patriarchal. Despite the fact that a woman was on the throne, she was, arguably, only nominally there as supreme ruler, as all her close advisers and confidants were men. Women, other than the Queen, had almost no legal rights to an existence which was independent of men. They were regarded firstly as the property of their fathers and after marriage, of their husbands. Upon marriage any property or land that was transferred with them in the form of a dowry became the husband's legal possession, to deal with and dispose of as he saw fit. The subjugation of the will and independence of the woman to that of the man is dramatized in the opening of Shakespeare's *A Midsummer Night's Dream*. While it is possible that Shakespeare is out of sympathy with this system (he does after all favour the lovers and makes it possible for them to be united), in this encounter he nevertheless reflects the prevailing attitude of his day.

In the plot of *A Midsummer Night's Dream* two young couples have been brought to the court of King Theseus at Athens to receive a judgement necessitated by conflict about a prospective marriage. The father of one of the women has been trying, unsuccessfully, to arrange for his daughter (Hermia) to marry Demetrius. She refuses, pleading that she loves another. As a result of this failure to obey her father she has been brought to court so her father may

> . . . beg the ancient privilege of Athens:
> As she is mine, I may dispose of her;
> Which shall be either to this gentleman
> Or to her death, according to our law
> Immediately provided in that case.
>
> (I.1.41–5)

89

The immediate response of authority to this plea is to remind the woman of her obligations:

THESEUS
What say you, Hermia? Be advised, fair maid:
To you your father should be as a god;
One that composed your beauties – yea, and one
To whom you are but as a form in wax
By him imprinted, and within his power
To leave the figure or disfigure it.

(I.1.46–51)

The law of 'Athens' was not the law of England in 1600: women could not be compelled to marry against their wishes. However, the spirit behind what both men say is representative of male attitudes towards women, because the real purpose of marriage at this time was *social*, not romantic. It was not concerned with legitimizing a sexual relationship in any spiritual or moral sense, but with ensuring that the product of that relationship – a child – could legitimately inherit the wealth of its progenitor. Romantic love as it is frequently portrayed today – a union of two people based on mutual attraction, often needing to overcome differences of wealth and status – was to all effects non-existent in Renaissance England. Marriage was primarily a business arrangement between the men of two families. In Shakespeare's England, women did ultimately have the right to refuse a marriage, but they had little practical alternative other than to live a life of seclusion in a convent or at home. As a woman you might turn down the offer of one man in marriage, but you could not, without great difficulty, turn down men and live independently of them. Thus Hamlet's advice to Ophelia, 'Get thee to a nunnery. Why wouldst thou be a breeder of sinners?' (III.1.121–2), is seen by him as her only alternative to marriage. There was no other social or economic structure to support a single woman, either physically or emotionally. Thus the dominant ideological (i.e. male) construction of femininity contended that a woman could only be fulfilled by marriage and motherhood. Consequently women were never seen as independent in their own right, but only as male appendages.

Because the primary purpose of marriage was to facilitate an economic rather than a romantic relationship, the virginity of the woman prior to marriage had to be established. Without this, any child born in wedlock might be suspected of being a bastard and hence denied the right to inherit the father's wealth. After marriage the same fear manifested itself as anxiety about being made a cuckold. This theme is almost universal in the drama of this period, not simply because it is seen to undermine the dignity of the husband and question his virility, but because it threatens social stability.

The focus on female chastity and fidelity pertained only to women who, because of their class, were likely to become suitable wives. Shakespeare makes this very clear in *Measure for Measure*. Where there is no economically significant relationship to protect, women exist to be used and abused as the male appetite dictates. We felt this was at the core of Touchstone's attitude towards Audrey, and in *Measure for Measure* much of the action and agonizing about the loss of Mariana's and Juliet's virgin status takes place in front of a whore-house where women are simply regarded as objects.

Many young people reading *Measure for Measure* today find incomprehensible the decision of Claudio's sister Isabella to refuse to give up her virginity in exchange for his life. It is easier to understand if we recall that without it she would have become a social outcast (Juliet and Mariana are both kept at a distance from society because they are unmarried non-virgins; non-people with no role and no future in life). Virginity was highly prized by men and, not surprisingly, highly protected by women. Male sexual desire had to be satisfied until marriage by the frequent use of whores.

Shakespeare sounds dire warnings about the dangers of uncontrolled pre-marital desire. In *The Tempest* Prospero warns the lovers Ferdinand and Miranda against the dangers of consummating their union too early. In a speech to Ferdinand, in which Prospero constantly refers to Miranda (his own daughter) in the language of the market place, he sounds a warning:

> Then, as my *gift*, and thine own *acquisition*
> Worthily *purchased*, take my daughter; but
> If thou dust break her virgin-knot before
> All sanctimonious ceremonies may
> With full and holy rite be ministered,
> No sweet aspersion shall the heavens let fall
> To make this *contract* grow; but barren hate,
> Sour-eyed disdain and discord shall bestrew
> The union of your bed with weeds so loathly
> That you shall hate it both . . .
>
> (IV.1.13–22, my italics)

The Tempest and much of *As You Like It* takes place outside the everyday social world. Ferdinand and Miranda are not in civilized Italy (although they are to return there) and Rosalind and Orlando and Celia and Oliver are not in the court, but in the forest (although they too will

91

eventually return to court). In a pastoral setting – an Arcadia on an island or in a forest – lovers are living in the natural world and are therefore supposed to be that much more close to natural desire. We can see this in the powerful and mutual sexual attraction of Ferdinand and Miranda, and we hear Prospero's warnings against consummating the relationship and satisfying the desire before the legal sanction of marriage has taken place. Prospero warns the couple because he knows, and they do not, that soon they will return to the social world where marriage is a public ceremony declaring both the legitimacy of the union and also that the woman is no longer available to other men. It is vital that there is no evidence (pregnancy) that could undermine the social status of the marriage or that of any subsequent offspring.

The power of desire and the need to bring it under control because it threatens to undermine socially legitimate marriage is graphically illustrated in *As You Like It*. The audience hear of the overwhelming physical attraction of Celia and Oliver. This, Rosalind realizes, must hasten the public ceremony of marriage, for their natural desire released in this natural place threatens their ability to return to the unnatural but, in masculine terms, necessary social and economic world.

ROSALIND O, I know where you are. Nay, 'tis true; there was never anything so sudden but the fight of two rams, and Caesar's thrasonical brag of 'I came, saw, and over-came'. For your brother and my sister no sooner met but they looked; no sooner looked but they loved; no sooner loved but they sighed; no sooner sighed but they asked one another the reason; no sooner knew the reason but they sought the remedy: and in these degrees have they made a pair of stairs to marriage which they will climb incontinent or else be incontinent before marriage. They are in the very wrath of love and they will together; clubs cannot part them.
(V.2.28–39)

Although sexual desire as illustrated here is presumed to be mutual, it was a widespread belief amongst men of Shakespeare's generation that once a woman had tasted the sexual act she would for ever after have an insatiable appetite for it. Married women, however chaste they appear, are frequently suspected of infidelity by their husbands (Desdemona in *Othello* and Hermione in *The Winter's Tale* are two obvious examples). Certainly any woman who was a widow was particularly suspect and considered especially dangerous. Widows were difficult for men to deal with because of their marginal position in society: they could (if they had been provided for by their husbands or family) live a life relatively independent of men. Having presumably had sexual experience, which could no longer be legitimately satisfied (i.e. within marriage), they became threatening because supposedly on the look out for more. Therefore they are made the object of jokes focused on their supposed lust for men. The power of the male ego to make myths that control the way in which women are seen is difficult to underestimate. Indeed if we go back briefly to *A Midsummer Night's Dream* and the response of the male authority figure (Theseus) to the independent aspirations of the female (Helena) we see that his idea of a punishment for refusing to obey her father's will is death *or* a life without sex; it seems that to him for a woman to live without a man is the equivalent of death!

HERMIA
>But I beseech your grace that I may know
>The worst that may befall me in this case
>If I refuse to wed Demetrius.

THESEUS
>Either to die the death, or to abjure
>For ever the society of men.

(I.1.62–6)

The threat posed to the male by female sexuality is seen as a potential loss of property – a possession exclusively owned and used is lost – rather than a mutual relationship broken down. This no doubt accounts for the vehemence with which men created a mythology about women's promiscuity. It helped subdue women by providing a rationale for their need to be controlled. The keystone of this practice is to make the woman always the guilty and therefore morally weak party. It is she who betrays the husband's trust and plants the dreaded cuckold's horns on his forehead. Men cannot cuckold women. In *As You Like It* it is quite clear that the threat comes from women and not from men. Rosalind, *speaking as Ganymede* to Orlando (i.e. one man to another) states that it is the cuckold's horns '. . . which such as you are fain to be beholding to your wives for' (IV.1.53–4). Likewise Jaques, the silent observer of the courtship of Touchstone and Audrey, remarks to the audience: 'Many a man has good horns, and knows no end of them. Well, that is the dowry of his wife, 'tis none of his own getting' (III.3.49–51).

The male fear of being cuckolded is seen in *As You Like It* as a necessary and inevitable part of being a man:

SONG

LORDS
Take thou no scorn to wear the horn,
It was a crest ere thou wast born,
>Thy father's father wore it,
>And thy father bore it,
The horn, the horn, the lusty horn,
Is not a thing to laugh to scorn.

(IV.2.14–19)

Critical Studies: As You Like It

In the culture and drama of the English Renaissance there is an uneasy co-existence of two contradictory images of women. They are seen as desirable objects to possess, but they are also a distinct threat to masculinity; given half a chance they will undermine the male and humiliate him. In the Forest of Arden, the paradise of Duke Senior contains no women to threaten male society with symbolic acts of castration. The likes of Phebe and Audrey have no contact with the Duke and his merry men. When socially significant women are finally introduced into the male sanctuary of Arden, there immediately begins the process of subduing and containing them by emotional and legal bonds.

Marriage, of course, was, and remains today, a legal bond. In Shakespeare's plays we see plenty of couples engaged in rapturous courtship. They look *forward* to marriage and in the comedies we are left to speculate how they will turn out. However, those marriages we do see could not be described as happy: Claudius and Gertrude, Othello and Desdemona, Leontes and Hermione, Lady Macbeth and Macbeth, and so on. In the actual marriage ceremony performed in churches during the reign of Queen Elizabeth I, the man was first asked by the priest if he would 'love her, comfort her, honour and keep her, in sickness and in health?' The woman was then asked (in this order) if she would 'obey him and serve him, love, honour and keep him, in sickness and in health?'[29] The promise to obey was subsequently repeated by the woman during the ceremony.

As You Like It contains two mock marriages. The first, between a 'fool' (Touchstone) and a 'foul wench' (Audrey), is solemnized by a false priest (Sir Oliver Martext). The second is between Rosalind/ Ganymede and Orlando, at which Celia is asked to play the part of priest. She has more scruples than Sir Oliver and is a reluctant player, unable to say the words completely. None the less, the ceremony mars the true text of legitimate marriage:

ROSALIND Come, sister, you shall be the priest and marry us. – Give me your hand, Orlando. – What do you say, sister?
ORLANDO Pray thee, marry us.
CELIA I cannot say the words.
ROSALIND You must begin 'Will you, Orlando'.
CELIA Go to. – Will you, Orlando, have to wife this Rosalind?
ORLANDO I will.
ROSALIND Ay, but when?
ORLANDO Why, now, as fast as she can marry us.
ROSALIND Then you must say 'I take thee, Rosalind, for wife.'
ORLANDO I take thee, Rosalind, for wife.

(IV.1.113–26)

Although the play ends on the point of a legal and legitimate marriage ceremony, the actual rite itself is only enacted in a context where its significance is mocked by false priests (Sir Oliver and Celia) and by participants, most of whom acknowledge their own duplicity. Similarly, the audience may be steered towards a sense of optimism for the future married life of two of the couples presented at the end of the action – Rosalind/Orlando and Celia/Oliver – but there remains the quartet of Phebe/Silvius and Touchstone/Audrey, for whom the future is doubtful.

Our production was interested in exploring the relationships between the two central 'female' characters in the play, for it seemed likely that if Rosalind's gender was unstable in relationship to Orlando, it would also vary when interacting with Celia. During the rehearsals this indeed proved to be the case, though problems about Celia's intended gender did arise. Because she is consistently presented to the audience as female, the actress playing Celia decided to accept her as such, even though she too would originally have been played by a boy.

Celia's verbal skills seem to be more a product of class than gender, and are in marked contrast to her physical weakness and inability to take action once in Arden. Any power Celia/Aliena has derives from her social status, not her gender; consequently it cannot survive outside the social world of the court. Celia is always in the dependent (i.e. feminine) role. She first depends on her father, then on Ganymede, and finally on Oliver. We also noted that Celia/Aliena is always on stage; she is often silent but none the less is there whenever Ganymede is present. Her presence helps to remind the audience of just how much a mutation this Rosalind/Ganymede actually is.

In the enactment of the Rosalind/Celia relationship, you can see demonstrated the reversal of the status and power within that relationship once Rosalind discards her false gender and reveals 'herself' as male. Studying the scenes at court reveals that it is Celia who is the dominant partner, both in terms of the amount of text she is given to speak, and also in the authority she displays by constantly taking the initiative in matters affecting the two 'women'. Her status derives from the fact that she is daughter to the current ruler. When the couple are first seen by the audience it is Celia who is first to speak. After the wrestling it is she who calls Orlando over to speak with Rosalind and herself. Following the bout, again it is Celia who takes the initiative:

CELIA

Gentle cousin,
Let us go thank him, and encourage him.
(I.2.227–8)

Critical Studies: As You Like It

When the angry Duke proposes banishment (ironically enough he attempts to justify his action by listing the very qualities in Rosalind that form part of the Elizabethan male's model of an ideal woman –'smoothness', 'silence' and 'patience') Celia proposes the flight from the court into the forest, and conceives how this may be accomplished in safety:

CELIA

Shall we be sundered? Shall we part, sweet girl?
No, let my father seek another heir.
Therefore devise with me how we may fly,
Whither to go, and what to bear with us,
And do not seek to take your charge upon you,
To bear your griefs yourself and leave me out;
For, by this heaven, now at our sorrows pale,
Say what thou canst, I'll go along with thee.

ROSALIND

Why, whither shall we go?

CELIA

To seek my uncle in the Forest of Arden.

ROSALIND

Alas, what danger will it be to us,
Maids as we are, to travel forth so far?
Beauty provoketh thieves sooner than gold.

CELIA

I'll put myself in poor and mean attire
And with a kind of umber smirch my face.
The like do you; so shall we pass along
And never stir assailants.

(I.3.96–112)

Thus we have the woman in the superior social role taking the lead and instigating the escape. Celia counters Rosalind's implied objections to the scheme and wins her over by enthusiasm and example. This sense of Celia's being in control is cemented in the audience's mind by having her deliver the departing lines at the end of Act I as much to the audience as to Rosalind:

CELIA

              ... Now, go we in content
To liberty, and not to banishment.

(I.3.135–6)

There is a real ring of optimism, even triumph, in these words. What a contrast to the next time the audience sees Rosalind and Celia. Then, in the fourth scene of Act II, Celia/Aliena has her femininity reinforced, but Rosalind appears now as Ganymede, and a man.

Ganymede initiates and controls the dialogue, while the first we hear of Celia/Aliena conveys not triumph, but physical weakness. Her tone is markedly different from her last speech. Now, instead of an *upbeat* proclamation, we hear a plaintive cry:

CELIA I pray you, bear with me, I cannot go no further.

(II.4.8)

At this point Celia is effectively ignored by both men (Ganymede and Touchstone) as they observe and comment upon the appearance of two others, Corin and Silvius. Even when this pair have left, she is still unnoticed until she breaks back into the scene by drawing attention to herself and to her condition:

CELIA

I pray you, one of you question yond man
If he for gold will give any food;
I faint almost to death.

(II.4.58–60)

In the exchange that follows, Ganymede stresses that Celia is now to be seen in relation to himself as the 'weaker vessel'; he uses *her* plight, rather than his own or Touchstone's to try to win assistance from Corin.

ROSALIND

Here's a young maid with travail much oppressed,
And faints for succour.

(II.4.71–2)

What the audience in the theatre is watching is the transformation of the previous female relationship to one between individuals of different sex. It is now the male Ganymede who is in control, while the 'woman' Celia is in need of protection and assistance. From now until the final moments of the last Act it will be Ganymede who directs events and manipulates both men and women.

The reasons given in Shakespeare's text for the women's decision to disguise themselves in their flight from the court is, according to Celia, because 'Beauty provoketh thieves sooner than gold' (I.3.108). But once they are safely arrived in Arden neither shows the slightest inclination to divest heself of her disguise. We suggested that it was necessary for Shakespeare to show this audience that the behaviour of Rosalind/Ganymede in Arden is appropriate to a male and not a female. As Ganymede, the boy-actor controls the wooing of Rosalind and Orlando. S/he is the teacher of the male, and thus in the dominant role – a total reversal of normal Elizabethan social convention. Likewise, as Ganymede, the boy-actor plays a role that carries with it considerable power to manipulate and control events. Independence of this kind was not a female virtue. Indeed Ganymede chastises Phebe for displaying just such independence. He attacks her because she has committed the unpardonable sin of asserting her will against that of the man who aspires to possess her. The country girl is castigated for refusing to play a role in a male fantasy of pastoral love. By saying 'no' she provokes a condemnation from Ganymede, couched in the terms known best to men – those of the exchange and market place: 'Sell when you can, you are not for all markets' (II.5.60). This attack is really quite savage. Ganymede implies that Phebe is physically unattractive to men and that her power comes only because Silvius is acting foolishly. The males close ranks when their dominance is threatened. In this way, Ganymede, while condemning the wilfulness of Phebe, praises Silvius. He is: '. . . a thousand times a properer man/Than she a woman' (III.5.51–2).

Phebe is not the only woman to be verbally attacked by men in the forest. Audrey is a character drawn to emphasize foolishness and gullibility. Her 'marriage' to Touchstone is treated as a joke at *her* expense. She has to be 'given' by Jaques to a man who is barely capable of concealing his contempt for her: 'Even a toy in hand here, sir' (III.3.70). The scenes involving Audrey may well produce laughter in performance, but it is laughter directed *at* her rather than laughter that comes from sharing an experience with her. Each of these male-manoeuvres can be seen as an attempt to contain the women by undermining their ability to act independently.

At the conclusion of the text in performance it was necessary for the audience in Shakespeare's theatre and the audience on the stage to witness the transformation of Ganymede back into the female role of Rosalind. (We noted that it is the one scene in the play which utilizes the whole of the acting company, bringing together figures from the pastoral world and that of the court.) Once the boy-actor is seen symbolically to discard his masculinity he must also be seen to leave behind the power and control he exercised as Ganymede. Shakespeare introduces the figure of Hymen (the god of marriage) in order that the bringing together of the couples – the active role – is not seen to be performed by a woman. When he returns dressed as a woman that control is transferred into the hands of male characters. Rosalind is now, as contemporary convention held befits a woman about to be married, passive and almost silent. Instead of the volubility of Ganymede, almost falling over himself with words and delighting in verbal combat, the audience now sees and hears a mature woman ready for marriage; a readiness demonstrated by the fact that she has only five more lines left to speak in the performance (other than the epilogue). The first of these is to her father, the second to her husband-to-be:

ROSALIND (*to the Duke*)
> To you I give myself, for I am yours.
> (*to Orlando*)
> To you I give myself, for I am yours.
> > (V.4.113–14)

This giving of herself and the demonstrable change from assertive to passive personality is part of the necessary public renunciation of independence. Portrayed as female Rosalind signals readiness to conform to the authority of the male world. She is now shown to be ready to return to the social world and take her appropriate place within it as the possession of a man. In Arcadia, in fantasy, you may go about in disguise and pretend to be a man, but in the real world women must be shown to acknowledge and willingly accept that their place is as the junior partner in the company of men. Rosalind is shown voluntarily to relinquish her previous role and enter into a 'natural' (i.e. man/woman relationship) as opposed to an unnatural one (man and man). She is now, at the end of the play, silent and still as the company prepare to return to the real world. It is all right to *play* at being a man just so long as it is recognized as play. In our production it was left to the actor playing Jaques to move slowly around the stage and speak lines that might well have been spoken by Ganymede: lines addressed *exclusively* to men:

> (*to the Duke*)
> You to your former honour I bequeath:
> Your patience and your virtue well deserves it;
> (*to Orlando*)
> You to a love that your true faith doth merit;
> (*to Oliver*)
> You to your land, and love, and great allies;
> (*to Silvius*)
> You to a long and well deservèd bed;
> (*to Touchstone*)
> And you to wrangling, for thy loving voyage
> Is but for two months victualled.
> > (V.4.183–9)

Finally, the boy-actor in the character of Rosalind comes forward to address the audience in the epilogue. Here, although superficially presenting himself in the female role, he none the less reminds the audience, as they are about to depart, that 'she' is now, and has been throughout, he:

If I were a woman, I would kiss as many of you as had beards that pleased me . . .
> > (V.4.211–12, my italics)

This chapter is not designed to provoke a whole series of performances of *As You Like It* in which the female roles are played by men. There are already too few good parts for women without denying them Rosalind/Ganymede. What it has tried to do is to illustrate that the question of gender is pertinent and interesting in this play, and that its presentation of women in the context of Shakespeare's contemporary time and place is not necessarily the same as modern performance and criticism has led us to accept as being authentic. This text certainly challenges that of the Romantic director. For him Rosalind was the embodiment of femininity; someone whom he could both recognize and idealize. This text, on the other hand, sees Rosalind as essentially masculine.

As with the political text, this production, or set of ideas that arose out of its preparation, generates questions about Shakespeare's intention and the problems of reading a play without tradition obscuring some of the issues it may raise. The student reading this director's article may respond to the play very differently, and wish to counter some of its assumptions; for instance, that the relationship between Orlando and Rosalind/Ganymede is at least covertly homosexual. Any refutation of this position would have to match this group's rationalization for its interpretation based on knowledge of Renaissance England and the conventions of the Elizabethan/Jacobean stage as well as textual evidence. This is the crux of reading any play. You may construct a different performance-text by making informed decisions through an alliance of your intellect and imagination. There still remain many ways of making a production in the theatre of your mind's eye which is both as *you* like it and also a legitimate interpretation, supported by what Shakespeare wrote. But no reading will be valid if it derives purely from gut-reaction or whim; there must be evidence and sound argument.

The bibliography which concludes this book will point you to some sources which should help to construct the kind of performance-text you find most valid and interesting. The more widely you read, the more informed will be your final conclusions and the less likely you will be to fall into the trap of reading with constricted vision.

Text in Performance

'Few things are so pleasurable as to be able by an hour's drive to exchange Piccadilly for Parnassus,' remarked Oscar Wilde following an outdoor production of *As You Like It* staged by wealthy amateur players at Coombe House, Kingston-upon-Thames in June 1885.[30]

As You Like It has always been a popular play, with both amateur and professional actors eagerly seizing the opportunity to enter into the spirit of Arden. In particular there seems to have been an urge on behalf of the performers to get the text out of the artificial surroundings of a theatre and into a genuine pastoral setting. Outdoor performances – despite the British climate – have proliferated over the years. Even the recent BBC Shakespeare series was persuaded to take the play out of the studio and into the grounds of Glamis Castle in Scotland, so that the viewers (presumably having taken their sets into their gardens) could observe Rosalind (Helen Mirren) and Orlando (Brian Stirner) 'fleet the time carelessly' in the undergrowth.

In the nineteenth century, outdoor performances positively flourished. When researching this book, I came across one in a *most* unlikely setting for anything pastoral: Denver, Colorado, USA. There, in the summer of 1897, the ladies of the 'Home Department' of the 'Women's Club' had organized a production which had 'the greensward as a carpet, the sun as the calcium to shine on the fairest of Rosalinds, and with overspreading trees for the love-sick Orlando to carve the name of his Rosalind upon . . .' In this setting the resourceful amateur cast played out a comedy to the delight of an audience dressed in 'brilliant summer attire'. The great thing about the whole effort as far as the enthusiastic critic of the *Denver Republican* was concerned was that 'there was nothing suggestive of the stage in the surroundings'.

But the nineteenth century, as well as having more than its fair share of productions *au naturel*, also saw what is now generally regarded as the first modern production of *As You Like*

It. Charles Macready produced the play at the Drury Lane Theatre in London in 1842–3.[31] His work is recognized as 'modern' because, despite an emphasis on the visual and spectacular (the pit contained a full orchestra which opened the proceedings with an overture from the first movement of Beethoven's 'Pastoral' Symphony), he restored to the actor a good deal of spoken text which it had become traditional to omit. None the less, Macready's scene painter, Charles Marshall, painted ten complete settings: Oliver's house in the orchard; the Palace exterior; a room inside the Palace; seven different locations in the Forest of Arden, including one of Rosalind's and Celia's cottage, one showing a sheepfold in the distance, and one called in the programme 'The Beechen Avenue'. What Macready was doing with *As You Like It* was very much in line with the fashion of the time. The technical limitations of the Elizabethan stage (with no stage lighting and limited technology) was seen as a handicap to Shakespeare's talent, and it was assumed, perhaps rightly, that had his company possessed the technical facilities and manpower of the mid nineteenth-century theatre in England, they would have made full use of them. In productions of the classics on the nineteenth-century stage, the imagination of the audience was frequently up-staged by spectacle. As one enthusiastic reviewer of Macready's *As You Like It* wrote:

... the scenery, and its adjuncts, supply to the outward senses some such images as appear to the mind's eye of the reader, we are ready to exclaim with Touchstone, 'Now I am in Arden'.

(The *Athenaeum*)

The critic from the *Spectator* gives a very interesting report of Macready's production which I want to quote at length because it gives a good picture of a performance in the context of the theatrical conventions of nineteenth-century Britain. Note what the reviewer finds significant to draw to the attention of his reader:

As You Like It was represented on this occasion as the poet wrote it, for the first time in the memory of the present generation of playgoers, and, it may be said without presumption, as he would have wished to see it represented – at least so far as scenic accessories are concerned. The spectacle is not merely correct and elegant, but suggestive; aiding the fancy in realizing the local and other characteristics of the dialogue. The architectural views are designed in the old French style; and the sylvan scenes have a wild and primitive aspect, denoting the remoteness and seclusion of that 'desert inaccessible', the Forest of Arden: old trees of giant growth spread their gnarled and knotted arms, forming a 'shade of melancholy boughs' for the banished Duke and his sylvan court; the swift brook brawls along its pebbly bed; the sheep-bells 'drowsy tinkling' is heard from the fold on the hillside; and the lodge in the wilderness, overgrown with creeping plants, is musical with birds ... The last scene, a stately vista of lofty trees, in which a floral temple is erected by the foresters to Hymen's altar, is a pretty fancy in pastoral taste. In short, nothing is wanting to complete the scenic pictures; nor is anything overdone.

To go to such lengths to create an illusion of reality on the stage may at first seem strange and have very little to do with what *As You Like It* may or may not be about. But therein lies a major difference between late twentieth-century conventions and those governing the staging of plays in mid nineteenth-century London.

In the second half of the twentieth century the academic and theatrical worlds have grown closer together. Criticism of Shakespeare now pays attention not only to more traditional literary concerns, but also to an analysis that takes account of the ways in which meanings are manufactured in performance. And in the theatre itself, those responsible for the creation of those meanings are themselves often the products of a university education which prizes analytical skill. The Royal Shakespeare Company currently work on the development of a performance-text in rehearsal over several weeks (a rarity in the nineteenth century, and unheard of in Shakespeare's day). Their practice gives priority to the exploration by the director – another twentieth-century innovation – and actors of the *ideas* stimulated through encountering a dramatist's text, and to finding an appropriate, significant, and exciting way of articulating them. The emphasis on excavating ideas from the text throws considerable responsibility on to the director-as-thinker, as well as on his or her abilities to generate and draw performances from actors. On the whole, in the late 1980s we expect to see a production of *As You Like It* that will be an 'interpretation' of the Shakespearian text; an interpretation usually based on the director's ideas concerning the play's significance at the time s/he first considered working on it. Indeed, I suggest we would be very surprised to visit Stratford, the

Barbican, or whatever venue, and see a production of *As You Like It* which to all intents and purposes emphasized the same themes and preoccupations as the last production of that play we saw. The search is always, it seems, to give a 'new' reading of the text, or at least to cast fresh light on an old and familiar work.

There are those who have argued that this process has gone too far, and that the presentation of classic drama, and of Shakespeare in particular, has become dominated by the concerns and preoccupations of the director, often at the expense of Shakespeare's own clear intentions. This argument to free Shakespeare from directorial distortion which seeks out novelty for its own sake, has not had a significant impact on the theatre practice of the last ten years or so. Indeed, the convention of production-as-interpretation cannot really change as long as the dominance of the director remains as absolute as it does today. There are very few signs of a shift in fashion back to the pre-eminence of the actor, despite at least one well-publicized and articulate cry against the 'directorcratic system' of theatre in Britain (Simon Callow's in *Being An Actor*).[32]

Like it or not, current theatre practice in staging Shakespeare is dominated by the influence of directors (and increasingly and interestingly of designers too) over the product – the performance-text – eventually consumed by audiences. I have previously quoted at length from a review of a famous nineteenth-century production of *As You Like It* in which (as in the outdoor performances) you saw a preoccupation with the physical environment in which the action of the spoken text is set. Macready's work was, you will recall, full of visual detail. I want to follow on from that and take an example of a production of *As You Like It* created more recently and use it to illustrate the tremendous change between the emphasis and approach of the 1840s and that of the 1980s. What follows is an examination of part of the Royal Shakespeare Company's prompt-copy of Terry Hands's 1980 production of *As You Like It* (extract from IV.2). Hands cast Susan Fleetwood as Rosalind, Sinead Cusack as Celia and John Bowe as Orlando.

Perhaps with another person reading out the actual spoken text, you could use a draughts board and, by naming the pieces as characters, recreate the movements on the stage. This would give you an idea of whether any given movement is purely functional (i.e. merely to get on or off the stage) or has, in addition, some particular significance in the action. Remember, *gesture* is a language in itself, so too is silence; the sign ⌒ indicates a pause — look out for them; they often reveal how the actor is interpreting what is being said. Remember too that many stage directions in modern printed editions of plays of this period are the work of editors and not necessarily an accurate indication of what the dramatist wanted.

The following diagram may help to clarify what is taking place on the stage and the abbreviations used to signify movement. The stage at Stratford (where the first performance of the production took place) is divided into eight sections by an imaginary grid. This enables the stage-management to plot the various movements of the actors on to, in, around and off the playing area. Thus a movement on the stage might be notated by the state management: Enter Ros. USL and Xs (crosses) to DSR and sits R of C (right of centre).

USR (Up Stage Right)	USL (Up Stage Left)
CSR (Centre Stage Right)	CSL (Centre Stage Left)
DSR (Down Stage Right	DSL (Down Stage Left)

PROS R
(Proscenium Right)

The line is CS
(Centre Stage)

PROS L
(Proscenium Left)

AUDIENCE

see other men's; then, to have seen much and to have

(1) nothing is to have rich eyes and poor hands.

JAQUES Yes, I have gained my experience.

Enter Orlando

(2) ROSALIND And your experience makes you sad. I had
rather have a fool to make me merry than experience to
make me sad – and to travail for it too!

ORLANDO

(3) Good day, and happiness, dear Rosalind!

JAQUES Nay then, God buy you, an you talk in blank verse. (5)
(*Going*)

ROSALIND (*as he goes*) Farewell, Monsieur Traveller. Look
you lisp and wear strange suits; disable all the benefits 30
of your own country; be out of love with your nativity,
and almost chide God for making you that countenance
you are, or I will scarce think you have swam in a
gondola. Why, how now, Orlando, where have you
been all this while? You a lover! An you serve me such
another trick never come in my sight more.

ORLANDO My fair Rosalind, I come within an hour of my
promise.

ROSALIND Break an hour's promise in love? He that will
divide a minute into a thousand parts, and break but a 40
part of the thousandth part of a minute in the affairs of
love, it may be said of him that Cupid hath clapped him
o'th'shoulder, but I'll warrant him heart-whole.

ORLANDO Pardon me, dear Rosalind.

ROSALIND Nay, an you be so tardy come no more in my
sight; I had as lief be wooed of a snail.

ORLANDO Of a snail?

ROSALIND Ay, of a snail: for though he comes slowly, he
carries his house on his head – a better jointure, I think,
than you make a woman. Besides, he brings his destiny 50
with him.

113

SOUND Q21 A 80

SOUND Q21B GO

SB LXQ26

LXQ26 GO

By delaying the entrance of Celia and also, slightly, that of Orlando, Terry Hands can add further emphasis to the Rosalind/Jaques encounter. Her decisive movement (1) is to tell Jaques that he will get nothing from her. The mood of frustrated and tense confrontation (a mood perhaps associated with love that fails to be reciprocated) is then changed radically by the entrance of Orlando and Celia; the change being marked by the pause before Jaques speaks his final

① Pushes herself away from him to DCR

② Slowly returns to R of him, on reft.

③ Orlando on pros R, Celia on pros L. They wave to each other, then Celia to C; Orlando picks flowers from CR + runs to L of Ros. He gives her the flowers then moves to R of her.

④ Kisses her on both cheeks.

⑤ Jaques Xs to DL then to UC, where he exits. Ros, Celia + Orlando move with him – Ros ends up L of Orlando, Celia US of the two of them

⑥ Jaques exits UC. Ros, Celia + Orlando wave goodbye to him. Ros + Orlando then laugh + turn to each other.

⑥a Orlando bows to Rosalind.

⑦ Throws flowers at him.

⑧ Turns away from Orlando + Xs to DS of DL stump.

⑨ Xs to R of her, Celia to C

⑩ Spins around to face him. Celia Xs to her shawl, picks it up, brushes it with her hand then puts it on

⑪ She advances on him – he retreats to DR.

⑫ Claps him on both shoulders.

⑬ " " " again, jumping up. He falls onto his knees, then she puts her finger on his forehead + pushes him into sitting position. He has one knee bent upwards –

⑭ He lies down on his back.

⑮ She sits on his bended knee + walks her fingers up his body to the top of his head.

line. The atmosphere on stage shifts decisively from a somewhat threatening encounter, darkly suggestive of rape, to one which is much lighter and more playful (the first thing Orlando and Celia do is to wave at each other like children). But before Rosalind and Orlando can freely indulge in their love-games, they must see off the dark figure of Jaques and wave him out of their lives. The laughter of Rosalind is at least in part the laughter that comes from relief.

The encounter being enacted in this performance-text stresses both a youthful playfulness and, at the same time, a recognition that the game is a sexual encounter (see move 7 and at what point in the spoken text it comes). It is also very witty. Remember that Celia, although a silent character at this point, is watching all that happens, and when she anticipates that the game is getting out

① Waves her fingers above his head
② Jumps to her feet
③ Falls onto him — he puts his arms out to catch her + they grapple at arms length. Celia runs to L of them + grabs Rosalind around the waist.
④ Pulls Ros US — Rosalind to UC, Celia to CL, Orlando stands DR.
⑤ Picks a flower from CR stump + puts it between her teeth.
⑥ Moves DS to C, Orlando to CR.
⑦ Lies on her back, head L, + opens her legs ∧ She then sits up to face Orlando.
⑧ Takes her hand + pulls her up to R of him

⑨ She Xs behind him to L of him, leaving her hand + flower R of him
⑩ Taps him on tummy with flower + moves hand to L of him
⑪ Very close to L of him
⑫ Turns from her + moves DS
⑬ Taps him on the head with the flower, drops the flower + marches US, F/E.
⑭ Collapses on the ground, head US, on his back. Ros rushes to US of his head + kneels.
⑮ Blows on his face to revive him. Celia sits L of them

of hand, she rapidly intervenes (move 3) to save herself and her cousin embarrassment. The *frisson* that is developed between Rosalind and Orlando comes because both push their roles almost beyond the brink which divides play from reality. Terry Hands is obviously keen to show that this is sexual foreplay.

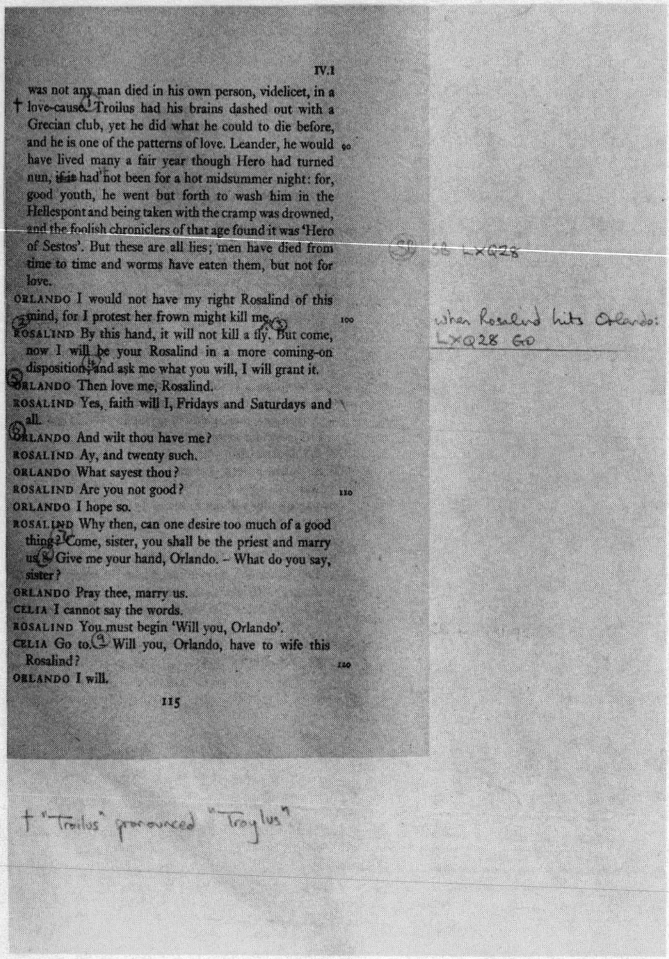

was not any man died in his own person, videlicet, in a
† love-cause. Troilus had his brains dashed out with a
Grecian club, yet he did what he could to die before,
and he is one of the patterns of love. Leander, he would 90
have lived many a fair year though Hero had turned
nun, if it had not been for a hot midsummer night: for,
good youth, he went but forth to wash him in the
Hellespont and being taken with the cramp was drowned,
and the foolish chroniclers of that age found it was 'Hero
of Sestos'. But these are all lies; men have died from
time to time and worms have eaten them, but not for
love.

ORLANDO I would not have my right Rosalind of this
mind, for I protest her frown might kill me.   100
ROSALIND By this hand, it will not kill a fly. But come,
now I will be your Rosalind in a more coming-on
disposition, and ask me what you will, I will grant it.
ORLANDO Then love me, Rosalind.
ROSALIND Yes, faith will I, Fridays and Saturdays and
all.
ORLANDO And wilt thou have me?
ROSALIND Ay, and twenty such.
ORLANDO What sayest thou?
ROSALIND Are you not good?   110
ORLANDO I hope so.
ROSALIND Why then, can one desire too much of a good
thing? Come, sister, you shall be the priest and marry
us. Give me your hand, Orlando. – What do you say,
sister?
ORLANDO Pray thee, marry us.
CELIA I cannot say the words.
ROSALIND You must begin 'Will you, Orlando'.
CELIA Go to. Will you, Orlando, have to wife this
Rosalind?   120
ORLANDO I will.

115

[handwritten note, right margin]: when Rosalind hits Orlando: LXQ28 GO

[handwritten note, bottom]: † "Troilus" pronounced "Troylus"

In performance, on move 3, Rosalind follows the movements of an imaginary fly buzzing around Orlando's head, finally swatting it on his stomach. The use of Celia's shawl, a property not specified in the printed text but added by the director, is made clear as this scene develops further. As well as acting as an altar-rail here, it later becomes a 'bedsheet' to cover the couple, and later still Rosalind

R C
O
|
|
|

① She leans on her L hand.

② Holds her R hand over his stomach

③ thumps him in the stomach & runs to UC. Celia stands Orlando jumps to his feet & picks up 2 poems – he makes them into horns & runs to DS of DL stump.

④ Orlando runs US to C, Rosalind runs DS to R of Celia & takes her shawl from her.

⑤ He charges at her like a bull – she dodges R, Celia runs to CL.

⑥ He charges again – she steps aside to L of him.

⑦ Spreads the shawl on the floor DC

⑧ Kneels on L edge of shawl, Orlando kneels on R edge of it. Celia to US of them. Ros takes Orlando's hand.

⑨ Hands together, chanting.

stands with the shawl around her like a bathtowel. As she releases it, it drops to the floor leaving her 'naked'. The next move in Terry Hands's prompt-copy directs 'Orlando looks at her body, and she momentarily covers herself up with her hands', which is followed by his spoken words 'Ay, sweet Rosalind.'

This is certainly a very bold treatment of one of the best-known scenes in the play. Some first-night critics thought it went too far. Certainly it has travelled a good way from Macready's production in which, in deference to Victorian sensibilities, all references remotely connected with sex were cut out: all talk of horns, words like bastard, or mistress, were substituted or omitted, and even relatively innocuous words had to go. Thus:

FIRST PAGE Shall we clap into't roundly, without hawking, or spitting . . .

(V.3.10–11)

became

FIRST PAGE Shall we clap into't roundly, without hawking, or coughing . . .

But Terry Hands and his actors were troubled by no such scruples. Rosalind is shown to be a 'tease'. But there is more to it than this, as Orlando himself (John Bowe) remarked in retrospect:

Terry's simple solution to lovers' games was circles: histories and tragedies have straight lines, comedies and romances have circles. If you had a map of our footprints in the two major scenes of the second half [III.2 and IV.1] you would have a picture of spirals all over the stage . . . In our production, the preceding Jaques/Rosalind scene [the beginning of IV.1] was played as a seduction by the melancholic intellectual of the vibrant youth (perhaps in an effort to complement his personality). So at the moment Orlando enters, Ganymede is on the verge of being devoured by Jaques and his cloak. No wonder she reprimands him. For me there was a definite shape to this, the second of the forest scenes. The games reach a crescendo when Rosalind gets Celia to marry them. 'I take thee Rosalind for wife', says Orlando in play and almost collapses in grief, as the despair of his unrequited love looms in his face. He looks at Ganymede and sees Rosalind. This happens again at the end of the scene. Rosalind encourages pretend bed-games based on their discussion of fidelity, and as Orlando makes to go she rises and, pretending that she is naked, drops Celia's shawl, which they have been using as a bedspread. Orlando is involved in the game, he almost imagines he sees his love's body. This is too much, the games must cease and he must leave, but Rosalind torments him and makes him promise to return at two o'clock, which he does, 'With no less religion than if thou wert indeed my Rosalind.' He has been wounded deeply and the next time they meet he has been wounded physically. Rosalind is cruel and he counters her curtly. She goads him and teases him about his love until he can bear it no longer: 'I can live no longer by thinking.' We all felt that it was at this point that Rosalind and Orlando learn their greatest lesson. He realizes that the dream is no substitute for reality, and she realizes that she has been very wrong to play with Orlando's emotions.[33]

By following the extract from the prompt-copy and looking at the moves and pauses, you will, I hope, have seen some of the extraordinarily detailed work that goes into making a contemporary performance-text. You will have seen that very little of what is printed has been omitted or changed, and that the stage directions have been used as a guide, but not followed slavishly. What we can see at work here – and it helps to read John Bowe's informative commentary on the events in which he played so crucial a part – is typical of the approach to transforming dramatic literature into a theatrical event adopted in the latter part of the twentieth century. You can see why contemporary companies need a six-week rehearsal period!

You may not *agree* with the Terry Hands's reading but I hope you can agree that his approach, and that of his actors, holds out the prospect of an exciting voyage of discovery. Above all, I hope this approach, and that of the book as a whole, illustrates that meanings are not generated solely in the mind of the dramatist, but are created and re-created through a collective, collaborative process which involves actors, directors, designers, audiences and readers. As an active reader you can and should make your own meanings. Lay claim to the text on your own behalf, as *you* like it.

Notes

Introduction

1. *The Empty Space*, pp. 12–13.
2. For a useful brief history of pastoral literature see Bryan Lough-rey's introduction to *The Pastoral Mode* (Macmillan Casebook Series).
3. Jonathan Miller, *Subsequent Performances*, p. 35.

1. A Dramatic Commentary

4. For a detailed discussion of this see my *Drama: Text into Performance*.
5. 'Let the Forest Judge', in *As You Like It*, A Casebook, ed. J. R. Brown, p. 163.
6. In Trevor Nunn's 1977 production of the play for the RSC.
7. See J. C. Trewin's *Shakespeare on the English Stage, 1900–1964*, pp. 85–7, Barrie & Rockliff, 1964.
8. For more details of this interesting production see Roger Warren's review in *Shakespeare Survey 33*, Cambridge University Press (1980), pp. 178–180. This journal produces an annual review of Shakespeare's plays performed by the RSC at Stratford.

2. A Romantic Text

9. See 'Let the Forest Judge' in *As You Like It*, A Casebook, ed. J. R. Brown, p. 153.
10. Chapter 9, 'The Alliance of Seriousness and Levity in *As You Like It*', p. 229.
11. Rosalind's description of a courtly lover also fits Ophelia's description (to her father) of Hamlet:

> My lord, as I was sewing in my closet,
> Lord Hamlet, with his doublet all unbraced,
> No hat upon his head, his stockings fouled,
> Ungartered, and down-gyvèd to his ankle . . .
> (*Hamlet* II.1.77–80)

12. See Harold Jenkins's article: 'As You Like It' in *Shakespeare Survey 8*.
13. Peter Brook's now famous productions of *King Lear* and *A Midsummer Night's Dream* were both influenced by Kott's work. See his chapters 'King Lear or Endgame' and 'Titania and the Ass's Head'.
14. *Shakespeare Our Contemporary*, p. 229.
15. Harold Jenkins, *Shakespeare Survey 8*, p. 43.
16. I quote Stephen Coote, joint-editor of the Penguin Critical Studies series, who has reminded me that the ideas in this speech would have been familiar to an Elizabethan audience. 'There was a considerable degree of discussion – arising principally from Seneca and Plutarch's *Morals* – as to whether man's life should be divided into five or seven periods. Shakespeare obviously opts for seven and gives us a familiar use of rhetoric in a speech which shows "what oft was thought but ne'er so well expressed". The [Elizabethan] audience would have been thoroughly aware of the rhetorical i.e. artificial, patterned and persuasive use of language here – a matter of central importance to all seventeenth-century drama.'

3. A Political Text

17. The author is the proud owner of a now empty box of '72 Shakespeare tea bags . . . Specially selected . . . *As You Like It*'!
18. See his *Theses on Feuerbach*.
19. 'All Things Bright and Beautiful', Mrs C. F. Alexander (1818–95).
20. Quoted by Harry Berger in the chapter 'Text Against Performance in Shakespeare: the example of Macbeth' – Stephen Greenblatt (ed.) *The Power of Forms in the English Renaissance*, p. 77, Oklahoma University Press, 1982.

4. A Feminist Text

21. Although there are some excellent directors who are women, they are in a minority and, at the time of writing (1987), none have directed a performance on any of the 'main' stages of the National Theatre or the RSC.
22. See *An Actor Prepares* and *Building a Character*.
23. For an interesting discussion of what happens when actors, directors and scholars read Elizabethan/Jacobean texts through a perspective conditioned by the performance conventions of psychological naturalism, see Alan C. Dessen's *Elizabethan Stage Conventions and Modern Interpreters*.

24. From Anna Seward's account of Mrs Siddons's Rosalind, a performance first given in the summer of 1786. See *Eyewitnesses of Shakespeare: First Hand Accounts of Performances 1590–1890*, ed. Gāmini Salgādo, p. 163.

25. See, for example, Toril Moi's *Sexual/Textual Politics: Feminist Literary Theory*.

26. See the actor John Bowe's account of the production and his role within it in Philip Brockbank's *Players of Shakespeare*.

27. See Michael Foucault's *The History of Sexuality, Vol. 1*, and Alan Sheridan's *Michael Foucault: The Will to Truth*.

28. *The History of Sexuality, Vol. 1*, p. 26.

29. *The Book of Common Prayer* (1552).

5. Text in Performance

30. See his delightful review of the performance in *Eyewitnesses of Shakespeare*, pp. 163–6.

31. Charles H. Shattuck gives a thorough and fascinating account of this production in his *Mr Macready Produces As You Like It*.

32. *Being An Actor*, p. 93.

33. *Players of Shakespeare*, pp. 73–4.

Select Bibliography

All quotations from *As You Like It* are taken from the New Penguin Shakespeare edition, edited by H. J. Oliver.

BARBER, C. L., *Shakespeare's Festive Comedy: A Study of Dramatic Form and Its Relation to Social Custom*. New Jersey, Princeton University Press, 1959.

BEVINGTON, David, *Action is Eloquence*. Boston, Harvard University Press, 1984.

BROCKBANK, Philip (ed.), *Players of Shakespeare*. Cambridge University Press, 1985.

BROOK, Peter, *The Empty Space*. London, MacGibbon & Kee, 1968.

BROWN, John Russell (ed.), *Shakespeare: Much Ado About Nothing and As You Like It*, Macmillan Casebook Series, General Editor: A. E. Dyson. London, 1979.

DESSEN, Alan C., *Elizabethan Stage Conventions and Modern Interpreters*. Cambridge University Press, 1984.

DOLLIMORE, J. and SINFIELD, A. (eds), *Political Shakespeare*. Manchester University Press, 1985.

DRAKAKIS, John (ed.), *Alternative Shakespeares*. London, Methuen, 1985.

FOUCAULT, Michael, *The History of Sexuality, Vol. 1*. Robert Hurley (tr.), London, Allen Lane, 1979.

HOLDERNESS, Graham (ed.), *The Shakespeare Myth*, Manchester University Press, 1988.

JARDINE, Lisa, *Still Harping on Daughters: Women and Drama in the Age of Shakespeare*. Brighton, Harvester Press, 1983.

JENKINS, Harold, 'As You Like It' in *Shakespeare Survey 8*, Allardyce Nicoll (ed.), Cambridge University Press, 1955.

KOTT, Jan, *Shakespeare Our Contemporary*, Boleslow Taborski (tr.), London, Methuen, 1965.

LOUGHREY, Bryan (ed.), *The Pastoral Mode*. Macmillan Casebook Series. General Editor: A. E. Dyson. London, 1984.

MILLER, Jonathan, *Subsequent Performances*. London, Faber, 1986.

MOI, Toril, *Sexual/Textual Politics: Feminist Literary Theory*. London, Methuen, 1985.

Critical Studies: As You Like It

REYNOLDS, Peter, *Drama: Text Into Performance*. London, Penguin, 1986.

SALGĀDO, Gāmini (ed.), *Eyewitnesses of Shakespeare: First Hand Accounts of Performances 1590–1890*. Brighton, Sussex University Press, 1975.

SHATTUCK, Charles H., *Mr Macready Produces As You Like It*. Illinois, Beta Phi Mu, 1962.

SHERIDAN, Alan, *Michael Foucault: The Will To Truth*. London, Tavistock Publications, 1980.

STYAN, J. L., *Drama Stage and Audience*. Cambridge University Press, 1975.

LIBRARY

F.... .eynolds was born in Cromer, Norfolk, in 1946. After leaving school he received professional theatre training at the Central School of Speech and Drama and at the London Academy of Music and Dramatic Art. He subsequently worked in the theatre in Britain and the United States before going to Sussex University to read English. He is now lecturer in drama at the Roehampton Institute, and lives in Lewes, Sussex. His publications include *Drama: Text Into Performance*, Penguin, and *Practical Approaches to Teaching Shakespeare*, Oxford University Press.